Light
to the
Darkness

LESSONS AND CAROLS:
PUBLIC AND PRIVATE

Light
to the
Darkness

LESSONS AND CAROLS:
PUBLIC AND PRIVATE

Katerina Katsarka Whitley

MOREHOUSE PUBLISHING

An imprint of Church Publishing Incorporated
Harrisburg – New York

Unless otherwise noted, the Scripture quotations contained herein are from the New Revised Standard Version Bible, copyright © 1989 by the Division of Christian Education of the National Council of Churches of Christ in the U.S.A. Used by permission. All rights reserved.

Morehouse Publishing, 4775 Linglestown Road, Harrisburg, PA 17112

Morehouse Publishing, 445 Fifth Avenue, New York, NY 10016

Morehouse Publishing is an imprint of Church Publishing Incorporated.

Cover art courtesy of Shutterstock

Cover design by Brenda Klinger

Interior design by Ronda Scullen

Library of Congress Cataloging-in-Publication Data

Whitley, Katerina Katsarka.
 Light to the darkness : lessons and carols, public and private / Katerina Katsarka Whitley.
 p. cm.
Includes bibliographical references.
ISBN 978-0-8192-2317-3 (pbk.)
1. Advent—Meditations. 2. Bible—Meditations. I. Title.
BV40.W478 2008
242'.332—dc22
   2008027194

Printed in the United States of America

08 09 10 11 12 13 10 9 8 7 6 5 4 3 2 1

To the memory of
Jane Heumann and Tracy Early.

You left us too soon, dear friends.

Contents

Acknowledgments

I owe an enormous debt of gratitude to the late Gerhard von Rad and his three books on the Old Testament that helped me understand the biblical promise from a new perspective. I bless his memory. I continue to be profoundly grateful to my Greek heritage, which from early childhood opened up the dramatic way of hearing and looking at stories.

I thank all those who have attended my workshops and retreats and have asked questions about the Bible. There is a hunger in many faithful people for understanding the unfolding purpose of God as revealed in the Hebrew and Christian Scriptures, but most of them don't seem to have that hunger satisfied in church. They long for deeper study but don't know how to pursue it. My books are written for them: to help them recognize the truth inherent in their baptismal vows and feel the excitement of the biblical stories as if for the first time. It is the interest I see in them that inspired me to write this book.

I thank my editor, Nancy Fitzgerald, for trusting the voices in my monologues and encouraging me to listen to them; and to Marilyn Haskell, music editor, for the selection of carols.

And again, as ever, I thank God for my father and my childhood communion of faith who nurtured me with these stories. And to my husband who lives with a writer—my thanks always.

Introduction and Stage Directions

There is a dialectic in Christian sacred art which impels it to stress, from time to time, now the eternal, and now temporal elements in the Divine drama.

—Dorothy L. Sayers[1]

The venerable tradition of *A Festival of Nine Lessons and Carols* emanating from King's College Chapel in Cambridge has delighted Anglicans in England since 1918; a decade later, thanks to the growing popularity of radio, the festival started reaching radio listeners worldwide, and soon it became popular with millions of Christians all over the world. Today, versions of *Nine Lessons and Carols* are lovingly performed in many parishes during Advent or on Christmas Eve. According to the program notes from King's College Chapel, the choice of the carols varies almost every year, while the "backbone of the service, the lessons and prayers, has remained virtually unchanged."

As with the magnificent *Messiah* by George Frederick Handel, whose libretto is based on biblical passages that unfold God's purpose from creation to the Incarnation and beyond, so the *Nine Lessons* follows a prophetic interpretation from Genesis to the birth narratives and the prologue of John's Gospel. The readings and singing have reached the level of a beloved ritual giving comfort and pleasure—as well as assurance—to the listeners. But as with all customs, familiarity often mutes the excitement of the story, and the loveliness of ancient and modern carols retains both nostalgia and freshness that often depend on the quality of the singers' performance. However, Old Testament passages in particular sound antiquated to ears of believers who reject a literal understanding of Adam and Eve as the first human beings who lived only six thousand years ago. And the story of the sacrifice of Isaac by his father Abraham, demanded by what agnostics deem a capricious god, sounds scandalous when divorced from the context of the times.

How do we retell these stories without doing harm to theology and without offending those who have moved beyond the "inerrant," quasi-"literal" interpretation of Scripture? The obvious answer for me is through drama. As the dramatist and brilliant lay theologian Dorothy L. Sayers writes in her introduction to *The Man Born to Be King*, "There is no more searching test of a theology than to submit it to dramatic handling; nothing so glaringly exposes inconsistencies in a character, a story, or a philosophy as to put it upon the stage and allow it to speak for itself. Any theology that will stand the rigorous pulling and hauling of the dramatist is pretty tough in its texture."[2] She goes on to say that the dramatist's intention should be "not to instruct but to show forth; not to point a moral but to tell a story."

This is my intention here—to allow the dramatis personae to tell the stories, within the unfolding of God's dream for those God created, from their own viewpoint, understanding, and interpretation.

I hope that the retelling of the stories in the form of the dramatic monologue will cause people to hear them as for the first time. This rediscovery of familiar stories, coupled with the traditional wealth of beloved carols, may cause young people (and adults, too) who may be unfamiliar with the biblical narratives to hear them for the first time. And it is my fervent prayer that those who have become so familiar with the text that they no longer hear it will be able to capture the eternal truth of God's love for all God has created as they enter the story. These are stories of human beings who lived in "the temporal element," but who understood something of the divine drama, of the eternal—people like Abraham and Isaiah, like Elizabeth and Mary of Nazareth, who were all convinced that God was a personal God. These are stories that matter to people like us. They are written in such a way that individual readers may use them for their own enjoyment and meditation; however, the stage directions, the inclusion of carols and hymns, and the form of the dramatic monologue make it possible for congregations of various sizes to stage them and enjoy them in community.

I state at the outset that I have followed the spirit, the truth of the stories, while allowing the imagination to change the text, to make it more approachable and understandable to listeners of the twenty-first century. The elegance, beauty, and tradition of *Nine Lessons and Carols* remain unchanged. This is simply another way to look at the same stories and

hear anew the carols that serve as the eternal *Yes* to the truth
that the stories reveal to us.

A WORD ABOUT THE CHOICE OF MUSIC

These retold lessons are offered to people of parishes and
churches of any size. I am aware that some enjoy the sounds of
tremendous organs and of large, well-trained choirs. Others
are limited by the size of the congregation, the instruments
they possess, and the number of singers in the choir. Size and
vocal training need not hamper the enjoyment of this service.
The carols and hymns may be sung by the whole congregation if there is no choir present. A combination of soloists
and group singing may also be substituted when a large choir
is not present. I am offering here, with the help of musician
friends, choices for large and small choirs and congregations.
The one prerequisite is that the monologues are read *aloud,
with the best diction possible, and with the required dramatic
interpretation.* I recommend that the speakers be spread out
in various places within the nave, with a stand and possibly a
lit candle in front of them; it would be effective to have the
nave lights turned off. These general stage directions are possible for all parishes.

For individual meditation during Advent, I suggest that
the reader be immersed in the music and the words as a form
of private prayer. Read one of the stories then listen to the
appropriate musical offering for a powerful Advent.

A Word about the Format of the Book.

Part I presents nine monologues in honor of *Nine Lessons and Carols*, together with suggested music and choral works. Each monologue is followed by an essay on the person of the speaker with occasional biblical commentary and historical background. These essays are for private meditation and study. They can also serve as preparation for the congregation before the performance of *Nine Lessons and Carols*. Each essay concludes with a spiritual exercise, so that the reader becomes a participant in the story, not just an observer.

Part II delves more deeply into the promise given by God and the movement toward the fulfillment of the promise and its final realization. It also visits the words of the prophets who offer what the church has agreed are messianic foretellings and assurances. My strong personal belief in the Incarnation runs throughout this section. Life for me would be meaningless without the Incarnation.

From my earliest years I responded to the drama in the biblical stories. My first attempt at writing centered on the person of John the disciple, and the creation of plays for my home church was my first intentional creative endeavor. You can imagine my delight then when I discovered Sayers' series of twelve radio plays called *A Man Born to Be King*. Intuitive preference transformed into intellectual and theological satisfaction. Seeing and hearing the stories has become an incarnational experience for me. I long to bring them alive in my writing also. As Sayers puts it most fittingly:

XVI LIGHT TO THE DARKNESS

From the purely dramatic point of view the theology is enormously advantageous, because it locks the whole structure into a massive intellectual coherence. It is scarcely possible to build up anything lop-sided, trivial, or unsound on that steely and gigantic framework. . . . A loose and sentimental theology begets loose and sentimental art forms. An illogical theology lands one in illogical situations. An ill-balanced theology issues in false emphasis and absurdity. Conversely, there is no more searching test of a theology than to submit it to dramatic handling.[3]

PART I

❊

Nine Lessons
and Carols

LESSON 1

⁂

Eve

Eve should speak like an old woman of wisdom and a great deal of humor—please, don't forget the humor! She is a storyteller with an immense store of knowledge and understanding. Please pay attention to the rhythm of the words. Do not rush.

It is no longer possible to remember how long it's been since we left the Garden—yes, well, as one of my great, great, great grandchildren reminds me—since we were *told* to leave the Garden. They ask me if I remember it. Of course I do. "Gardens are lovely," I tell them, "but we cannot live in them forever." (At my age, you can say anything and get away with it.) The children, so many I cannot count them, laugh uneasily. They sense that I have asked them here for a purpose. I have called them to draw close to me and they have gathered from near and far to hear my secret. I have been mulling over this for a long, long while. Here it is.

My Children, know this:

First, I have not minded so much leaving the Garden because God, blessed be his holy name, has never abandoned us. We may no longer have that sweet first contact, but we have been aware of the Holy Presence throughout this long time. *God has never abandoned us.*

Second, I know the stories that are being told among you; I hear them. You have some of it right and some of it so wrong it makes me laugh. But it does not matter. What does matter is that you understand this one great truth I have learned in my life: *having knowledge, even at the expense of leaving the Garden, has been worth it.* For it is through this great gift of knowledge that I have understood something of the Creator's power—yes, even the Creator's love. Out of what seemed punishment, came a great good; out of physical pain, all of *you* have emerged. The pain has been forgotten while the pleasure of your presence endures. Adam and I have known joy—how would we have tasted it had we not known its opposite, sorrow? And we have seen how darkness is dispelled when light arrives, night and day, after night and day. We never tire of it.

This is the secret: Out of *you*, maybe tomorrow, or maybe eons hence, God's promised fulfillment will arrive. You will not be left orphaned and abandoned. God created us in love. God will save us with love. Trust me and go in peace. Now that I have told you, I too am ready to leave this earth, *this* garden.

THE CAROLS

Anthems

"As truly as God is our Mother," William Mathias (Oxford University Press)

"Adam lay ybounden," Boris Ord (Oxford University Press)

"Adam lay ybounden," (unison) Peter Warlock (Oxford University Press)

"When long before time," David Cherwien (Concordia)

Hymns

"A Song of True Motherhood," *Enriching Our Music 2* (Church Publishing, pp. 177, 178)

"Of the Father's love begotten," *The Hymnal 1982* (The Church Hymnal Corporation, #82)

A MEDITATION ON EVE: WHO WAS SHE?

The man called his wife's name Eve,
because she was the mother of all living.

(Genesis 2:20)

One must see the man's naming of the woman as an
act of faith, . . . an embracing of life which as a great
miracle and mystery is maintained and carried by the
motherhood of woman over hardship and death. . . .
Who can express the pain, love, and defiance contained
in these words?[4]

Let's face it. She is one of the most verbally abused persons in
the Bible. Men have blamed her for everything that has gone
wrong in humanity's long history and women have apologized
for her. I wrote Eve's monologue originally for a church in the
United Methodist tradition. The woman who commissioned
me to write it was shocked at my interpretation of humanity's
foremother. When I asked her to examine the reasons for her
reaction, she said, "I wanted Eve to be sad, to be repentant."
Both of us were emotional over the issue. I was upset by *her*
statement, which seemed utterly unfair toward the person of
Eve. She was distressed by what I had written.

Obviously, even women disagree on their understanding of this first-named woman: some see the Genesis story as a magnificent, compact, theological retelling of God's act of the creation of the world and of human life, others see it as the historic account of a specific man and woman created, together with the universe, during a specific period of time. Yet those who cling to a literal interpretation miss the point. I have observed in many years of reading and listening that the most passionate defenders of this viewpoint often don't seem to know just what the Hebrew Bible says. I've realized—after countless conversations with believers and non-believers—that those who argue most vociferously have learned their position through the words of others, not through their own reading and study of Scripture. The more literary are influenced by John Milton's poetic retelling of the creation story in *Paradise Lost*, while others grasp on to the words of their preachers or, worse, their politicians.

Two Writers; Two Creation Stories

We cannot speak of the Creation or of Eve without looking at what biblical scholars have told us about the story. Recent scholars have concluded that Genesis 1—the Creation of the world—was written by a masterful writer who has come to be known as the Priestly writer, or as we shall call him, P. Gerhard von Rad writes of this first chapter: "Nothing is here by chance; everything must be considered carefully, deliberately and precisely." He calls this chapter the Priestly writer's "doctrine."[5]

The second Creation story, Genesis 2:4b–25, von Rad calls "the Yahwistic story of Paradise," and its writer, scholars agree, is very different from P; he has come to be known as the

Yahwist, or J, for the German *Jahweh*. Understanding the difference between the two versions helps us to see the story—and Eve—in a new way. So let's look at the biblical accounts.

First, let's remember that translations often are not accurate. Many misunderstandings have resulted from the difficulty of rendering Hebrew words—which contain no vowels—into another language. Take, for example, the Hebrew words *adam*, which means "of the earth," and *adamah*, which means "the earth," or "dust of the ground." Both words are impossible to translate exactly into English. Translating from Greek into English has been problematic, too. Using the earliest Greek version of the Old Testament, known as the Septuagint, some translators have rendered the Greek word *anthropos*, which means "human being" and applies to both genders, as *man*. But Greek, like Hebrew, has entirely different words for man and woman: *anēr* and *gyne*. So to say that God created *man* is to mistranslate the word and misunderstand the story.

Here's what Genesis 1:26a has to say: "Let us make a human being in our image, according to our likeness. It doesn't say, "Let us make *man* in our image. . ." as the King James Version declares. A modern translation, the New Revised Standard Version, corrects that mistake by translating it as "Let us make humankind in our image and in our likeness."

Let's look a littler farther on, in verse 27: "And God created *adam/anthropon*, in the image of God, he created him; *male and female* he created *them*." The change from the singular pronoun *him* to the plural *them* poses a puzzling problem. But one thing is clear. The writer declares that male and female human beings were created at the same time—not man first and later woman.[6]

Second, let's separate the first creation story in Genesis from the second one. Confusion happens when the two creation stories—the first from chapter 1 and the second from chapter 2—are conflated. It is this *second* story that most people think of when they speak of the creation of Adam and Eve, and it is the *first* story that they think of when they speak of the creation of the earth and the sea and all that is within them. Most people don't realize that they are two different stories written at different times by very different interpreters of the oral and written traditions. In this second story, man and woman are not created on the sixth day but *adam/anthropos* is created first, before all else. God makes *adam/anthropos* out of the earth and blows life into him. Then all the plants and living creatures are created to keep *adam* company and give him nourishment. Finally, woman is created so that man will not be alone: "And the Lord God said, 'it is not good for *anthropon* to be alone; I will make for him a helper just like him'" (Genesis 2:18). The NRSV writes of the "helper as partner," while the Authorized Version writes of *man* and the helper, *help meet* (something that doesn't mean much to modern ears). I find the Greek—*like him*—much more persuasive with its suggestion of equality and mutuality.

It is in this second story that the Garden of Eden is described. It is here that Adam alone is told "from the wood of the knowledge of good and evil you will not eat." But when Eve eats of the fruit and then offers it to Adam and he eats, he does not remind her of the injunction against eating it. So on whom does the blame fall? The decision is made by both of them. The word *sin* is never mentioned.

Looking carefully at what the story of Genesis really says shows the harm that has been done to women as a result of misreading, mistranslating, and misinterpreting the first two chapters. When we consider the abuse heaped on women in the past and the suffering of women in so many parts of the world today, we realize with a shudder that this is very serious—and enlightening—indeed.

Two Expressions of Eve

Though I don't consider Eve to be a specific, historic woman but All-Woman, I still thrill at the expression "daughter of Eve," which I first encountered in the writings of C. S. Lewis. As Eve is an expression of God's creation, of God's understanding of our need for companionship and love and pro-creation, I find myself a grateful part of this created order when I hear the expression "daughter of Eve."

The other expression that has caused me hours and hours of thinking and gratitude are these words from Genesis 1:26: "Let us make *anthropon* in *our* image of God, in *our* likeness," which I take to mean the hosts of heaven that surround the Creator God. I remember vividly the moment this understanding came to me. I was still very young, teaching a creative writing class to high school seniors, and I said without forethought—as if it came to me like an epiphany: "This is why we write, we paint, we sculpt, we compose music—we are created in the image of God; we are given the gift of creativity. God started it, Eve continued it by giving birth, and here we are millennia later giving thanks for this gift." Years later I was delighted to find confirmation in Carol Meyers' interpretation of Genesis 4:1–2a, "where Eve is said to have 'created a man together with the LORD.'"[7]

Thanksgiving to Eve and for Eve
Eve, you are woman,
wife and mother.
Above all, you are mother.
In you, mother Eve,
we honor mothers, we honor women.
We thank your Creator who made you equal
with man and gave you the gift of birth and nurture.
You worked hard beside the man tilling the soil
but you struggled even harder giving birth.
Love helps you forget the pangs of birthing.
Love urges you on to offer food, to give nourishment
to those who come near you,
to give knowledge to those
who seek it.

Creator of Adam and Eve, we thank you for Eden—
for the cool, green earth, for the beasts of the field and
    forest,
for the winged creatures that lift our hearts with joy by
    their
soaring flight and their song . . .
For the sounds of water, the rivers that flow, the sea
with its rich surprising life;
for all that forms our paradise, we thank you.
For the gift of the tree of knowledge and the
awe that fills us when we understand what is good
and can choose the difference from evil.

God of the universe, of Eden, of this good earth,
of our forefather Adam and foremother Eve,
We offer our thanks.

A SPIRITUAL EXERCISE

Write your personal letter or poem to Eve. Write a prayer to God thanking the Creator for all that you notice in creation that fills you with gratitude. Make a commitment to preserve the earth put in our trust.

LESSON 2

Abraham

Abraham is very old and utterly resigned. His life has been lived with all its triumphs and tragedies and mistakes, but this one event remains the most vivid in his mind, and in talking about it he finds an answer that satisfies him. Still, the memory remains truly terrible. The voice should be that of an old man, rather gravelly, sad, but, at the same time, full of hope.

Sarah says I've lost my mind. She says that this is not how our God deals with us. "Just because we are surrounded by fools who think their gods are after blood, you think *our* God is the same," she yells at me. It's easy for her to talk about this now, when Isaac is alive and safe, his hand firmly clasped in hers. I don't think she'll ever let him go. I don't think she'll ever trust me with him again.

My son. God's promise. The child of my old age. My hope and my terror. I was so sure it was *God's* voice I heard telling me to take him to the hills that I did not hesitate, though my heart bled. I didn't say anything to Sarah; she would have killed me with her bare hands had she known. My son and I traveled for three days and Isaac, sweet and obedient as was his nature, didn't ask questions until the very end. "We have everything we need for sacrifice, except for the animal, Father. Where is the animal for the sacrifice?" And I, unable to lie to him, said, "The Lord will provide."

The Lord *did* provide. I keep asking myself: Would I have done it? *Could* I have done it? Killed my own child? All the neighboring tribes do this—they sacrifice their firstborn to honor their gods. How could I do less than the pagans? Do I love Yahweh less than they love their gods? Is this what I was thinking? I no longer know. But Sarah is sure *she* knows. She thinks I feel so guilty about abandoning Ishmael, my other son, my true firstborn, that I felt compelled to sacrifice Isaac. Sarah has no patience when it comes to Ishmael and his mother, Hagar. Maybe she's right. I have never stopped thinking of them. I have never forgiven myself.

But my God has forgiven me—this I know. Isaac has forgiven me. I had tied him on top of the sticks of wood, on a frame I built while my hands shook and my eyes poured out their tears, and he only looked at me as if to say, *Even now I trust you, Father.* This is what I was saying in my mind also: *Even now I trust you, Yahweh.* And it was then that the angel of the Lord stopped my hand from committing the crime. Sarah scoffs: "It was fear of what I would do to you that stopped you, you foolish old man," she says, but her voice trembles with the imagined horror of it all.

So I have to ask myself, *Whose voice was it I heard? How can God make promises if God intends to take them back?* I am beginning to wonder what it is that we men call the voice of God. Now, when my life is nearly spent, I am sure only of those true moments when the call of God to me was clear, beyond all doubt. That moment when God called me out of Haran, and I obeyed. And later, in the darkness, out of my deep sleep, when God's promise came to me that my descendants would be blessed, that they would know God. This I have believed and this is the God I have obeyed. No matter what Sarah says, what will be remembered about me is that I believed in God's promise even when nothing around me gave any proof that the promise would be fulfilled, even when the fulfillment of the promise was demanded and almost snatched from me. Even then I trusted Yahweh. Even then I trusted Yahweh.

THE CAROLS

Anthems
"God's Promise," Samuel Adler (Oxford University Press) (SSA)

"In dulci jubilo," 14th-century German, arr. R. L. dePears-all, ed. R. Jacques (Oxford University Press)

Hymns
"The Song of Zechariah," *Wonder, Love, and Praise*, #889, #890

"Sing, O sing, this blessed morn," *The Hymnal 1982*, #88

A MEDITATION ON ABRAHAM:
THE TERRIBLE SACRIFICE

And I will make of you a great nation,
and I will bless you, and make your name great,
so that you will be a blessing. (Genesis 12:2)

The promise given to Abraham has significance, however, beyond Abraham and his seed. God now brings
salvation and judgment into history... a source of universal blessing.[8]

Being painfully familiar with the plight of the Palestinians
and the historic agonies of the Jews makes me enter the
Abrahamic realm with fear and trembling. At a time of war in
Iraq and terror in the Middle East and elsewhere, I am aware
of the claims the three major monotheistic religions make on
the person of Abraham. My father, who taught me so much
about faith, adored Abraham for his trust in and obedience
to the Lord, but I have found Abraham a difficult man to
like. Yet, I am grateful that the stories and sagas about him
are brutally honest, so that he appears to us with all the weak-
nesses of humanity despite his giant status as the father of the
religions that claim him.

I will set aside the question of historical accuracy. Some of the stories are sagas and a few concerning Abraham have the whiff of legend about them, but they reveal the essential truth proclaimed by the ancient Hebrews that God acts through and in history, that he is a God of promises, and that Abraham was a man of obedience. I grew up with the stories of Abraham and all of Genesis and Exodus. My father read biblical stories to us every night of our childhood years and they became part of me as the Greek myths were part of me from a forgotten dawn of awareness. Abraham and Sarah were part of our faith story, so it is difficult now to remember a time when they did not matter.

When my father told us the Old Testament stories, he did not leave any of the hard parts out. Questions were inevitable and he always tried to answer them. What I came to regard as "the easy answer" was this: *God has his reasons. What we don't understand now, we will one day.* As a child I believed this, but that doesn't mean that I gave up on the questions. What I could not forgive, however, no matter how it was explained to me, was the call for the sacrifice of Isaac. It angered me and saddened me, and my brother still teases me that Dad had to stop his reading because I dissolved into tears, and he could not continue to upset me. The stories of the sacrifice of Isaac and of Joseph's abuse by his brothers were so painful that I still remember running away to another room in order not to hear them.

So, as you see, this has an emotional connection to me intensified by the powerful effect of childhood memories. Abraham mattered and the stories still matter. Yes, he was obedient to God; yes, he was willing to leave everything that was familiar and set out toward the unknown to found a new nation in a new place—and for that he is admired and revered. Still, he lied about his wife and he took advantage of other people. His treatment of Hagar and Ishmael seems unforgivable to me. But he is the great man of faith, and who am I to question him? But oh, the story of Isaac!

I couldn't quite enter into the enormity of it when I was young, even though, to a child, the comfort of having Yahweh produce a ram in place of the almost-slain Isaac was tremendous. The *deus ex machina* was a familiar Greek theme: Euripides used the same kind of substitution in the story of the preparation for the Trojan war, in his *Iphigenia in Aulis*. A daughter about to be sacrificed is replaced by a deer. Agamemnon, the chief king among the many Greek kings, responds to the prophecy of Calphas, the seer, by sending for his daughter to come to Aulis on the promise that she is to be married to Achilles. All the Greek ships are waiting for the propitious winds to carry them to Troy, but the winds refuse to stir. The king lies to his wife, Clytemnestra, saying that he has made marriage plans with Achilles for his first-born daughter, even though his intention is to sacrifice her in order for the gods to allow the winds to blow favorably. It was a horrible deception and he eventually paid with his life for his willingness to sacrifice his child.

The Greeks, from time lost to us, were so offended by human sacrifice that they changed all the myths that hinted at it to something different. Euripides, writing in the fifth century, gives us the more merciful version of the substitution. The Trojan war is supposed to have happened in the thirteenth or twelfth century before the birth of Christ; the

Isaac story probably happened in the eighteenth or sixteenth century before Christ. It hurt me to listen to the story of Iphigenia and it hurt doubly so to hear the story of Isaac—after all, one was mere myth and the other was the Bible!

The stories of Abraham and the patriarchs were collated and written much later—some as late as the sixth century BCE—when the writers understood much more clearly and deeply the role of Yahweh in the history of Israel and the world. The Jews, also, had rejected the human sacrifice practiced by some of their neighbors, but the emphasis of the sacrifice of Isaac deals with Abraham's willingness to obey God, even though this request went totally against the promises given to him by the same God. And therein lies the wonder of Abraham's trust: he believed in the God of promises, *even when the promise was snatched from him in the most violent way.*

For me this story is the best example of the meaning of that loaded word *context.* I use the telling of the almost sacrifice of Isaac to unfold the word's multiple layers with my students. When did it happen and when was it first written down? Who wrote it? Who were Abraham's neighbors? What else do we know about that second millenium BCE? These questions help my students to lift the story from the literal to the realm of wider meaning: What is the writer telling us about God? Why does it matter? And, to my great satisfaction, they get it.

A SPIRITUAL EXERCISE

Try to think of a time when God seemed to be capricious in your own life. Were you ever at a place where you felt that "all was right with the world" only to have your joy or contentment snatched from you? Did you ever feel that God did not keep a promise to you? Write about this memory or experience and tell God what this felt like, what your disappointment tasted like.

Lesson 3

Miriam

Miriam is a strong woman who has lived through hardships, who has felt jealousy and anger, but who loves her brother despite all his faults. She spends much time living in her memories. She has had her doubts, but now they are resolved. Despite everything, she trusts Yahweh completely.

"It is the law that matters above all else," my brother Moses says, and maybe he's right. Moses is always right; the one time I said he wasn't, I was exiled from the community of the people. So now I try to listen to him and nod.

This is certainly quite different from the days of his infancy and childhood, for I could do no wrong then. My mother, as she nursed him, told him that he would not be alive had it not been for me, and he treated me like his savior for many years afterwards. He loved me and he admired me.

Those years are forgotten by everyone but me now. I still see in the prematurely white-haired man he has become—this worried, harried man who tries to lead the ungrateful people—I still see in him that little boy I rescued by letting the Egyptian princess see him in his adorable infancy.

How I loved the child! Rescuing him made me responsible for him and he looked to me for love and guidance more than he looked to our own mother. So, after he left the palace and came back to us, I thought it would be the same between us—I would be the elder sister and he would listen to me as the people do, most of the time.

But Moses is sure that he listens only to God. And again, I think he is right. God *does* favor him. When this reality first penetrated my brain, I felt such an intense jealousy I almost lost my mind. How I longed for God to talk to me as God talks to Moses! After that first triumph at sea, when Pharaoh's army was finally vanquished and we were free to roam toward the promised land, I thought I would help Moses lead the people. But little by little I was pushed aside and he became the one and only leader of the people who, almost always, resent him, abuse him, and come crying and yelling for help only when everything else is going wrong for them.

I have finally understood that they don't want a leader. What the people need, what they long for, though they are not able to realize it, is this: they want a savior, a rescuer, someone to carry their burdens; and, perversely, someone to blame when all goes wrong. That's not who Moses is; he is their leader, not their savior; that's why they resent him.

And he, in the wisdom he has acquired after much suffering, knows his place. He tells them that their liberator, their deliverer, is God and only God. But they quickly forget this.

The moment Moses' back is turned, they make their own saviors out of gold and stone, just as the pagans do. Desperate and angry, filled with sorrow, Moses asks God for help. Yahweh offers them the covenant through Moses together with the commandments that help them keep the promise. "It's the law that matters," he tells them again and again. And still they long for a savior. "Who will come to rescue them?" I ask God, I ask Moses. "As long as they are disobedient, they will never find out," Moses says. He asks God for a sign, some kind of assurance, and God leads him to a high mountain to help him look into the fulfillment of Yahweh's promise. I too long to see the fulfillment of the promise, but even though it may not be granted to me, I trust in the God of the promise; I always trust in the God of the promise, in the covenant God made with us.

THE CAROLS

Anthems
"From east to east, from shore to shore," from *Six Christmas Songs for the Young*, Malcolm Williamson (Boosey and Hawkes)

Hymns
"From east to east, from shore to shore," *The Hymnal 1982*, #77

"Miriam's Song," *Voices Found*, #15

"O little town of Bethlehem," *The Hymnal 1982*, #78, #79

A MEDITATION ON MIRIAM:
HER ROLE IN TRIUMPH, IN EXILE

And Miriam sang to them:
"Sing to the LORD, for he has
triumphed gloriously;
horse and rider he has thrown into
the sea." (Exodus 15:21)

Contrary to the impression that her one stanza sung at the sea is but an abridgement of the lengthy song attributed to Moses, historical and literary studies show that the latter version is itself the Song of Miriam.

It belongs to a corpus of women's traditions that include the long Songs of Deborah and Hannah.[9]

I have been fascinated by Miriam ever since I wrote about her in *Speaking for Ourselves*.[10] I realized then, and later, how little attention the church pays to her. Sunday school children have an image of her as a little girl peering through the reeds on the shore of the Nile, trying to see what happens to her infant brother hidden in the basket that flows down the river. And there we stop.

Years ago I wrote a midrash on Miriam—a retelling of the story as it is found in Exodus, but I didn't stop there; I moved on to the terrible chapter in Numbers 12 where she complains to God about Moses. She complains in tandem with her brother Aaron, but only *she* is punished by Yahweh for turning against Moses. She is stricken with leprosy and sent into exile. The storytelling in that chapter is masterful: imagery is vivid, the details sharply edged. Yahweh comes down in "a pillar of cloud" and stands at the entrance of the tent. Yahweh speaks with Moses "mouth to mouth" and not in dreams and visions as with the other prophets. Yahweh makes it plain that Moses is his favorite among them.

Scholars tell us that this is a very, very old story, but when it was written during the monarchy years, sometime between the eleventh and sixth centuries BCE, there was probably a dispute about the role of Moses, or a dispute about the priestly superiority of the Levites, and the writer wanted to make it absolutely plain that there was no greater prophet and leader than Moses and his legacy. The description of Moses as the "meekest" or most "humble" of men is also suspect; one can tell that this is a story that promotes Moses' supremacy as God's chosen mouthpiece. I have no trouble with these details. What has concerned me in this story is the attitude toward Miriam, a woman and a prophet. We learn so much about the prevailing attitude toward women when we pay attention to the details.

The most obvious injustice is that Miriam is punished because she complained against Moses, but Aaron, who joined her in the complaint, is not. Miriam is not only stricken with "leprosy" but is exiled from the community. Moses intercedes for her, but Yahweh likens her punishment to that of a father spitting on his daughter—a terrible disgrace equal to a curse.

So I spent time exploring this shameful punishment by writing what—I didn't know at the time but learned later—was a midrash. Old Testament scholar Walter Brueggemann describes a midrash this way: "A type of Jewish exegesis that tends to focus on elements in the text that do not accommodate themselves to any smoother or larger rendering." He elaborates: "The work of midrash is to exercise enormous interpretive imagination, so as to give visibility and emphasis to precisely what is nearly invisible or pointedly deemphasized in the text."[11] This is exactly what I longed for for Miriam—to give her visibility and to reveal her pain. I wanted Miriam to have a voice, to tell me what she felt about this injustice against her.

I wrote the story from her perspective, but I was not satisfied. Years passed and the monologue was included in *Speaking for Ourselves*.[12] I asked myself: What do women do with suffering, with injustice? How do they cope? How have they endured so many injustices and injuries through the ages, all because of their gender? I am convinced that there have been exceptions throughout the ages of women who did not acquiesce to their low status. I am a great believer in exceptions, and Miriam, the first recorded woman poet, prophet, and leader, could not possibly have accepted her position. How did she transform it? Miriam is punished because she is jealous of Moses—that's what the story tells us. "Has not the Lord also spoken through us? Has he not spoken through us also?" And then, I looked into my own heart.

What made *me* jealous was not so much the injustice of growing up in a society that favored men over women but *the privileges that men took upon themselves as favored by God over against women who, in their minds, were much less favored.* That rankled. And that also caused the terrible sickness of jealousy. What did Miriam do with that jealousy of God's favor to Moses? And then it came to me that the mere thought of it was an acknowledgement of sin. Once she acknowledged her jealousy, she was free of it. Then, I think, she must have been grateful for the seven-day exile from the loud, exhausting community; in the midrash her exile became a gift, like a spiritual retreat. The writing of that particular midrash on Miriam helped me understand much about myself as a woman of faith.

Miriam is the first woman to be called a prophet, probably an early use of the term referring to ecstatic praise. She led the women with dance and song and is obviously the poet who created the song known, unfairly, as "The Song of Moses" (Book of Common Prayer, 85), instead of as "The Song of Miriam".

Epiphanies come unannounced to surprise and bless us. I had not thought seriously about the portrayal of women in Scripture until that moment when I read Numbers 12 and felt anger at the injustice done to Miriam. Then I realized that the acceptance of these stories, without questioning them, had caused untold harm to women through the ages. I believe that my writing on biblical women comes from a profound longing to correct this injustice.

A SPIRITUAL EXERCISE

Have you ever felt injustice because of your gender? Have you ever felt that you were punished unfairly by God or a parent? Write down your hurt and offer it up to God so that it may be taken away from you and be healed.

LESSON 4

David

This is the young David, before he became king, before power and wars changed him. He is full of love for life and for Saul, whom he wants to save from despair. David should have a lyre near him, visible to the audience. He is charismatic and irresistible in the portrait of his youth, and that should be evident in the presentation.

I stood in that huge dark tent and tried to focus on the single beam of light slipping in from the angled roof. My eyes, at home only in the bright outdoors, finally found the brooding shape of Saul. He stood leaning on that rough piece of wood that held up the tent, that led to the light, as if he couldn't stand without help. Imagine—that tall, strong man that towered above the Hebrew people, unable to stand on his own.

Where was the king I had admired?

He had disappeared inside a shell of darkness because he had stopped trusting the Lord.

I felt a strong shaft of compassion for my king and tears stung my eyes. I lifted my right hand and strummed the strings of my lyre. Words of love for Saul and praise for the goodness of the Lord arose from within me and sang their way from my mouth to Saul. I sang of love, I sang of joy, I sang of the beauty of the earth, I sang of *life*!

Saul, imprisoned in the darkness of his soul, still kept his chin resting on his chest. I had been singing for hours before he finally stirred and shivered mightily. It was as if he were breaking chains and would emerge free. Brimming over with hope, I kept on singing for hours, until his son Jonathan, taking pity on me, approached his father and put his arms around him. Jonathan motioned for me to depart.

Every time the darkness came upon Saul I was called to the tent or to the palace. On a few of those visits Saul would emerge from his prison, but on others he would slip further into his fear of death that, for me, turned into fear for my own life. He knew that I had been called by God to succeed him, but Saul could not accept this. I struggled to think only of him, to love him and honor him as my king. I cried to God, "I will give up my hope for a kingdom, if you will restore Saul to his true self."

When Samuel, the prophet, heard my cry, he took me aside. "David, it is you who are now God's anointed. Yahweh has turned his back on Saul. God has blessed you and the house of David will be blessed. Accept the blessing."

And I did as Samuel told me. "Oh Lord God, you are God, and your words are true, and you have promised this good thing to your servant; now therefore may it please you to bless the house of your servant, so that it may continue forever before you, for you, O Lord God have spoken and with your blessing shall the house of your servant be blessed forever" (2 Samuel 7:28–29).

THE CAROLS

Anthems
"Lo, how a rose e'er blooming," by various composers

Hymns
"Lo, how a rose e'er blooming," *The Hymnal 1982*, #81
"While shepherds watched their flocks," *The Hymnal 1982*, #94, #95

A MEDITATION ON DAVID AND
THE ROYAL COVENANT

The crowds that went ahead of him and that followed
were shouting,
Hosanna to the son of David!
Blessed is the one who comes
in the name of the Lord!
Hosanna in the highest heaven!

(Matthew 21:9)

The stories about David, the young shepherd and later warrior king, read like novelettes in the two books of Samuel. He is a fascinating character—no one can deny it. Sunday school children may know more about David than any other character in the Old Testament because the stories about him are reminiscent of heroes from Greek mythology. Who has not heard of the adventure of David versus Goliath, and the young David's triumph? Who has not heard, in some allusion, the story of David's seduction of Bathsheba?

The David narratives are very old. To understand them better we must remember that he lived ten centuries before the birth of Jesus, but the collating and writing of them took place during a long period—the seventh and sixth centuries

BCE—from both oral and written traditions. There are overlapping stories about the prophet Samuel, about tragic Saul's rise to power and his reign, and about David's huge struggle toward ascendancy to the throne and the brief joining of the two nations, Israel and Judah.

But we understand history and historical writings very differently from the way of the ancients. Even the Greek writer Herodotus, who is called the father of history, mixed facts with fantasy and legend. The ancient Hebrew writers were not so much concerned with provable facts as with God's guidance and God's mighty acts in history as these related to God's covenant with the people. Their interpretation therefore is theological and, according to scholars, the narratives about David are examples of the earliest such writing: They teach and explain God's involvement and God's acting through history. God's promises to Abraham and his descendants continue through the ages but find a different focus with David. God's covenant now becomes *personal* to David and his line, not just to Israel/Judah. David is seen as the fulfillment of the promise. Even a cursory reading of Saul's and David's reigns reveals that history has been unfair toward Saul and very favorable toward David—highly troubling elements in the stories. Brueggemann uses strong words for this favoritism: ". . . Yahweh is inordinately and irrationally committed to David."[13] He is even more pointed later: "David can do anything he wants, because David is linked to Yahweh in modes of acceptance and affirmation heretofore unavailable in Israel and certainly unavailable to Saul."[14] Although monarchy is established in Israel against God's will for his people, God blesses David and does not withdraw his blessing despite his sins. Yet, when poor Saul repents of his own sins, God's face is turned from him. What does that say about Yahweh, who elsewhere is reported to be "no respecter of persons" (or, as the NRSV puts it in Acts 10:34, "shows no partiality")?

The stories about the time of monarchy that covers half a millennium are fraught with the struggle of the people to remain obedient to God's teaching; the teaching that came to them through the prophets. The stories are also filled with the people's repeated and tragic failure to remain obedient. Eventually, the monarchy proves to be a failure both politically and religiously. Throughout these vividly told stories, David stands as the king who defines Israel and her connection to God. He is important to us because, above all, he is a flawed human being who remains faithful to God. Thus David the king is also David the religious poet who loves God. To Jews and Christians, David was—and remains—an inescapable, towering figure.

And one reason he's so important is that we identify him with "God's anointed," or the Messiah. David starts his life with great dignity, with loyalty to Saul, and with self-sacrifice. He serves Saul, who wants to kill him, but he never retaliates against his king. He is charismatic, gifted with acclaimed musical and poetic abilities. It is later in life, after David becomes king, after his many military battles and victories, that he starts to deteriorate morally. After his adultery with Bathsheba and the murder of her husband that he instigates, there is distinct evidence of dissolution and failure. His life does not end in honor. Israel recognizes David's failure, especially in not securing a worthy successor. Solomon, for all the legends, is a failure before God. Thus, after the monarchy passes, the people of God look for a "new David," a true Messiah and deliverer.

It was the Christian church that identified Jesus as the second David. The Gospels point to Jesus as David's descendant, and the birth narratives of Matthew and Luke place his birthplace in Bethlehem, David's hometown. The Gospel of Matthew begins: "An account of the genealogy of Jesus, the Messiah, the son of David, the son of Abraham." In the same chapter, the angel of the Lord calls Joseph "son of David" also. Luke puts it this way: "Joseph also went from the town of Nazareth in Galilee of Judea, to the city of David called Bethlehem because he was descended from the house and family of David" (Luke 2:4).

David is the great grandson of Ruth and Boaz of Bethlehem. His name is mentioned eight hundred times in the Old Testament, sixty in the new. Bethlehem, as his home and the birthplace of Jesus, is a significant connection for Christians.

David is a character I grew up with. I cannot remember not knowing about him as a child. He was as attractive to my young imagination as Odysseus; it was only as an adult that I started seeing the darkness in both David and Odysseus— the cunning, the duplicity, the love of military might and achievement in battle.

I like David as a young man, a shepherd, and an artist. I like what Michal, Saul's daughter, saw in him when she first married him.[15] But I don't like him in his later life. Military might and the trappings of the palace seduce and ruin him. Little by little, the house of David crumbles. And yet, and yet. . . . The testimony of the people of faith is that David is beloved of God. His faults are not hidden from us. His sins are displayed for all to see, and David is not hesitant to admit them and repent before God.

What is of greater interest yet is the testimony of the prophets who refer to David repeatedly. The covenant of Moses was made with all of the people of God. But now the covenant is made only with the house of David, the royal covenant, and that endures for centuries. The people were convinced that a new David would save them. And the church is convinced that a descendant of David is the Savior in the person of Jesus the Christ. This is why we cannot think of Advent without mentioning David. His legacy endures.

A SPIRITUAL EXERCISE

Can you think of people in history (or in a more personal way, in your own life) who, despite their own failings, did (or continue to do) good to others? It is beneficial to remember that God does not choose only holy people to achieve God's purpose; sinners and even agnostics have been used by God to fulfill God's promises. That includes each one of us. Does that give you hope?

LESSON 5

✳

Isaiah and His Wife

Isaiah is an aristocrat—impressive and rather dreamy—with a voice like a French horn. The quotes at the beginning and within the piece must be spoken with a voice that is filled with the vision, uttered differently from the rest of the dialogue. The wife is young, obviously in awe of her husband's powers, but perfectly able to deal with his visions.

Isaiah: *(in a dreamy voice)*

A shoot shall come out from
the stump of Jesse,
and a branch shall grow out of
his roots.
The spirit of the Lord shall rest
on him.... (Isaiah 11:1–2a)

37

The wolf shall live with the lamb. . . .
And a little child shall lead them. . . .
The nursing child shall play over
the hole of the asp,
and the weaned child shall put
its hand on the adder's den. . . .
They will not hurt or destroy
on all my holy mountain,
for the earth will be full of the
knowledge of the Lord
as the waters cover the sea. (Isaiah11:6–9)

Wife: Oh, Isaiah, oh, how beautiful your words are! What are you seeing? Why is it that the rest of us cannot see such lovely visions of peace?

Isaiah: *(as if waking up from the sweet vision)* The Lord called me, and I am willing to go. As I prepare to proclaim his word, the visions arrive, but even I cannot live in them.

Wife: I am almost glad, Husband, because I could not follow you if you entered this peaceable kingdom; how could I? How can anyone?

Isaiah: Ah, my dear wife. I enter the vision only as a dream. I am a man of unclean lips in a nation of sinful people. Now, I am being commanded to go, to warn the people of their sins. *(Pause. He lifts his hand as if to shield his eyes; the light changes to denote another location.)* Woe is me, I am lost, for I am a man of unclean lips.

Wife: Look, Isaiah, can you see? Is this a seraph? Is this whom the Lord sends together with your visions? He is touching your lips, Isaiah, be careful! Oh, no, is that a live, burning coal? I cannot bear to look. . . .

Isaiah: *(in a different kind of voice)* He has removed my guilt. *(In a louder voice)* "Here am I, send me!"

Wife: *(as though telling a story that had been interrupted)* And so I lost him again, for days, for weeks, for months. He called out to the people to

> Cease to do evil,
> learn to do good;
> seek justice,
> rescue the oppressed,
> defend the orphan
> plead for the widow. . . .

Isaiah: But they fail to obey the Lord. They fight, they make war, but Yahweh has shown me, and I proclaim to them that they cannot accomplish anything on their own. Yahweh is supreme, filled with righteousness and justice.

Wife: The years pass. Isaiah moves between joy and despair; for years he remains silent. And then I and our two sons hear his voice again, triumphant, like the sounds of a trumpet.

Isaiah: Thus says the Lord:

> The people who walked in
> darkness
> have seen a great light . . .

(together they intone)

for unto us a child is born,
unto us a son is given,
and the government shall be upon his shoulders;
and his name shall be called
Wonderful Counselor
Mighty God
Everlasting Father
Prince of peace.

THE CAROLS

Anthems

"For unto us a child is born," from *Messiah*, G. F. Handel

Hymns

"Isaiah the prophet," *Wonder, Love, and Praise*, #723
"In the bleak midwinter," *The Hymnal 1982*, #112
"Song of Hosea," *Enriching Our Music 1*, #86, #87

A Meditation on Isaiah of Jerusalem

The people who walked in
darkness
have seen a great light . . .
(Isaiah 9:2a)

The preaching of Isaiah represents the theological high
water mark of the whole Old Testament. . . . Not one
of the other prophets approaches Isaiah in intellectual
vigour or, more particularly, in the magnificent sweep
of his ideas.[16]

Let's look at the first part of the book of Isaiah, the prophet
who lived in the eighth century BCE. Scholars have known
for a long time (at least from the eighteenth century CE)
that the second half of Isaiah was written later, in the time of
the Persian King Cyrus, who reigned in the latter part of the
sixth century BCE, and some of the chapters are later still. So
there were two prophets—and possibly more—writing under
the same name. The First Isaiah, or Isaiah of Jerusalem, saw
visions, wrote, spoke oracles, and cried out during the critical
time of the latter half of the eighth century BCE, when Israel
(the northern kingdom) was annexed by Assyria, and Judah,

the small southern kingdom, paid tribute to it. Isaiah prophesied in the southern kingdom at approximately the same time that Amos and Hosea prophesied in the northern kingdom.

Isaiah is a poet of undisputed greatness; his imagery and use of language are on par with the highest literary achievement of other nations and cultures—the Greek Homer (almost a contemporary) comes readily to mind. But what Isaiah knows about the character of God is so far above all the guesses of other poets of Near and Middle Eastern nations that comparisons fail. Isaiah was the first prophet to proclaim true monotheism; other gods simply don't exist for him. He was utterly convinced, and remained consistent in his faith, that Yahweh is the one who determines the course of history. He places his utterances in specific times and specific places with a sanity and a clarity of vision that startle us today. There is little doubt that he prophesied in Jerusalem, that he had ready and easy access to the royal court, that he must have belonged to the aristocratic or priestly class, but always his sympathies lay with the poor and the oppressed. We know when he lived because of the references to the kings: the end of Uzziah's life, the reigns of Jotham, Ahaz, and Hezekiah. The books of 2 Kings and 2 Chronicles refer to Isaiah also in their historical accounts of these four kings. Uzziah was mostly faithful to Yahweh but did not abolish the high altars of the old gods, so he was punished with leprosy; as a result he hid from the people. The uncleanliness of the king may have affected the people also; thus Isaiah refers to himself as a man of unclean lips until he is made pure by the fire of God. Uzziah's son Jotham, though otherwise a man of God, made the same mistake: he did not remove the high altars to idols. Ahaz was openly disobedient to God, making alliances with pagan nations, acts that enraged Isaiah; Hezekiah did much better, except for his flirting with foreign alliances also.

A second shining conviction that permeates First Isaiah is that Yahweh is holy: he is worthy of the highest praises, of glory. Only Yahweh possesses unquestioned moral purity. Isaiah refers to Yahweh as "the Holy One of Israel" who practices justice and righteousness. The author of First Isaiah sees universal implications in Yahweh's reach to all nations: salvation is not reserved for Judah alone.

In the monologue I took poetic liberties. It has been suggested that Isaiah was a priest; this is why when the vision comes he is inside the Temple. However, I wanted to give a chance to his wife, "the prophetess," as he calls her in the book, to witness the seraph's act with the burning coal, one of the most vivid images in Isaiah. That Isaiah did not hesitate to obey the call of Yahweh is the reality I cling to. That his calls to repentance fell on deaf ears is a reality that is repeated throughout history. Isaiah's glorious visions did not come to pass; his oracles were not fulfilled in his lifetime. Isaiah is a peacemaker whose visions thrill us to this day and make us long for the peaceable kingdom. It is his tragedy and ours that the peaceable visions of one who abhorred military power and the shedding of blood have not come to pass. Yet he remained faithful to a God of holiness and righteousness. He never fails to inspire us, to give us hope, to fill us with the need to cry "Glory!"

SPIRITUAL EXERCISE

Commit yourself not to just reading the Bible but studying it with the help of commentaries. The most readily available help is found in the Bible itself, specifically the New Oxford Annotated NRSV, which offers a wealth of notes and references. I always refer to the footnotes and read all of the cross references given for a certain passage. You will be amazed at the interconnectedness of Scriptures. So start with this exercise. Then, if your interest grows, you may want to consult a dictionary of the Bible. (I use *The Interpreter's Dictionary of the Bible*, volumes 1–4.)

LESSON 6

※

Malachi

An unassuming prophet who announces the coming of the forerunner, Prodromos, the one the church recognized in John the Baptist. Malachi is rather severe, filled with his gift of prophecy, which is the only thing that gives him comfort and assurance. He looks like a rabbi, probably with a head covering.

"See, I am sending a messenger to prepare the way before me, and the Lord whom you seek will suddenly come to his temple, even the messenger of the covenant whom you delight in. . . ."

(Malachi 3:1)

My name is Malachi, which doesn't much matter because it is not the name that was given to me at birth. I am called Malachi because the people perceive that I am *God's messenger*. Throughout our long history, we have called God's messengers *angels*—we the people of God who live in the lands of Israel and Judah. But it is not an angel that I see in my visions, but a man. Sometimes he is called Elijah, sometimes simply God's messenger. My calling is to announce his coming.

I keep a constant conversation with the Lord God of hosts. I ask questions and the Lord answers me. Then the Lord asks questions of the people, but the people have no answers.

They have drawn far from their Maker because again and again they forget the covenant God made with his servant Moses. I grieve for the people. I grieve for the heart of God because I perceive God's sorrow at the unfaithfulness of his people. I keep thinking of the day of judgment, the last day. It fills me with fear for us all. I know the words of the prophets who have gone before me, all that they have said about the day of the Lord.

"Make straight in the desert a highway for our God," Isaiah had cried out, but no one heard him.

"What does the Lord require of you but to do justice?" Micah had asked, but only he himself answered.

"Let justice roll down like waters, and righteousness like a rolling stream," Amos had prayed, but he returned to his flock disheartened.

And now it is my turn to proclaim the day of the Lord's coming, the great and terrible day of the Lord. But before that day of judgment comes, I ask Yahweh to have mercy on his people. Tell them this, the Lord God promises: "Return to me and I will return to you. . ." and then, "See if I will not open the windows of heaven for you and pour down for you an overflowing blessing."

I run to the people to bring them this message of hope. I beg them to listen, and those who still revere the name of the Lord do listen; the Lord has pity on them and blesses them. From then on the promise of a new messenger has stayed with me and never leaves me. Thus says the Lord: My messenger "will turn the hearts of parents to their children and the hearts of the children to their parents so that I will not come and strike the land with a curse" (Malachi 4:6).

I do not know the day or the time, but I have been given this assurance: "The one who is to make ready a people prepared for the Lord *will* come!"

THE CAROLS

Anthems
"A babe is born all of a may," 15th c., William Mathias (Oxford University Press)

Hymns
"The great forerunner of the morn," *The Hymnal 1982,* #271, #272
"Herald, sound the note of judgment," *The Hymnal 1982,* #70
"People look East," *Wonder, Love, and Praise ,* #724
"People look East," *Voices Found,* #34

A MEDITATION ON MALACHI

I have loved you, says the LORD.
But you say, "How have you loved us?"

(Malachi 1:2a)

There are three things that make the prophet Malachi distinctive:

1. He is the last of the Twelve Prophets.
2. His book is the last in the Old Testament.
3. He is the only Old Testament writer who speaks of a forerunner, a messenger, before the final advent of Yahweh.

The author of this fascinating book is actually anonymous. Malachi, after all, is not a proper name; it probably means "my messenger" and was added, somewhere along the way, by an editor. The book, likely written in the middle of the fifth century BCE, after the Babylonian exile, presents six oracles that speak against current practices or abuses, both social and religious. Malachi is passionately against divorce and very upset by the indifference and casual attitude of the priests in their liturgical duties. Malachi wrote during a time of skepticism and doubt when the people—the returned exiles—see that Yahweh's promises for deliverance foretold in the beautiful prophecies of Second Isaiah have not been fulfilled. With bitterness, they have drawn away from the sure faith of their ancestors as uttered in the prophetic voices of old. They live under occupation by the Persians and they suffer from natural disasters. The implied question that is painfully present in the literatures of most people during war and suffering—"Does God care for us?"—runs throughout this book. Other nations blame Fate, or their own arrogance, or the indifference of their gods. But the Hebrews were used to thinking that Yahweh was on their side, always, no matter what they did. Skepticism of this nature is not found in the Hebrew people's response to their God before this particular time—the insult of exile and the bitter disappointment of return.

The returned exiles don't have a written code of behavior yet—it will arrive much later, with the laws of Ezra and Nehemiah; eventually it will become codified and hardened into a kind of fundamentalism that will lead to the Pharisees' attitude during Jesus' time.

Malachi is not considered one of the major prophets, but he contributed greatly toward a more elevated concept of the sacred duty of the priests and emphasized that the union between husband and wife was sacred. He also recognized and declared that a pure sacrifice was acceptable to God no matter where it was offered, which prepares us for Peter's declaration in Acts 10:35: ". . . but in every nation anyone who fears him and does what is right is acceptable to him."

For the Christian, Malachi's greatest contribution is the foretelling of "the one who goes before to prepare the way."

Malachi saw this as the arrival of the angel of Yahweh on the day of the Lord. But Jesus told his disciples quite clearly that Malachi was foretelling the mission of John the Baptist, whom Jesus calls Elijah according to the prophecy: "Elijah has come and they did to him whatever they pleased." The early church accepted without hesitation that the connection of John to the messianic mission of Jesus was the perfect fulfillment of the prophecy of Malachi. Quoted by Mark at the beginning of his gospel and by Luke in the words spoken by the angel Gabriel to Zechariah, John's father, and by Zechariah himself in his great hymn we know as the *Benedictus*, the passage on the forerunner has become an integral part of the Christian story.

In the liturgy there are phrases and passages that move us deeply. Without fail the familiar sentence, "Blessed is the one who comes in the name of the Lord," brings me to tears. It is for me that moment of recognition when the divine touches me. In the Greek this benediction contains the meaning of continuous coming: I love that meaning. The one who comes in the name of the Lord comes to us regardless of our state. Oh, if we would only recognize the messenger and offer welcome.

A SPIRITUAL EXERCISE

Did a certain person or event bring you to the knowledge of God's love in Christ? Write this down as a thanksgiving poem or prayer to the one who was sent to you, the one who is continually coming to meet you.

LESSON 7

✵

Zechariah and Elizabeth

Zechariah, a priest, should be dressed rather formally for the circumcision and the naming of the child. Elizabeth is also in her finest robe because this is a special occasion. If at all possible, some of the audience should be in on this and react with awe and sighs according to the words of the couple, as marked in the script. This is a dialogue of joy.

Elizabeth: Zechariah, my beloved husband, the hour has come. Look, the house is filling with people and there is a crowd standing outside the door. I have told them that our son's name will be John and they are astounded. "But no one in your family has that name!" they are protesting, and what they are saying is correct. So why am I so positive that this is the name that must be given to this baby of our old and blessed age?

You have been silent for nine months now. They have been good months of quiet but also of much joy. Remember when Mary came to see us? Remember the delight we both felt and how the baby danced in my womb at her approach? *(Zechariah smiles and nods his head as she speaks.)* I think I have understood you most clearly, Zechariah, during these months of silence, even though you have not spoken aloud, and I have a vivid picture in my mind of the visit of the angel to you as you served in the temple. Together with you, I have been filled with awe and the greatest anticipation. And now the child is with us, the circumcision has been performed as our Lord commanded, and we are all waiting for you. Has the hour come at last?

Zechariah: *(In sign language he motions for a tablet and a piece of chalk. The tablet can be slate like that used in kindergartens in bygone days and the chalk can look like a piece of stone. Someone from the congregation hands them to him. Zechariah writes a name in large letters and lifts it up. A huge "Ah!" escapes the assembled people when they see the name JOHN. Zechariah then lifts both his arms up and speaks. If the actor is up to this, he can start a bit hoarse—since the voice box has not been used in months—and proceed, gradually getting clearer and louder.)*

Blessed be the Lord God of
Israel,
for he has looked favorably on
His people and redeemed
them.

He has raised up a mighty savior
for us
in the house of his servant
David.

(Zechariah now brings his arms down and looks at the baby before him. This of course is done without an infant present. The direction of his gaze and his eyes will denote the presence of his child. His voice changes, becomes very tender.)

And you, child, will be called the
prophet of the Most High,
for you will go before the Lord
to prepare his ways,
to give knowledge of salvation to
his people
by the forgiveness of their sins.
By the tender mercies of our God,
the dawn from on high will
break upon us,
to give light to those who sit in
darkness and in the shadow
of death,
to guide our feet into the way
of peace.

Elizabeth: *(wipes tears from her eyes)* Ah, Zechariah, I have never heard you speak so beautifully. You sound like a prophet; *(with surprise)* you *are* a prophet, my husband. But what does it all mean?

Zechariah: *(as if still prophesying)* He will go before the Lord to prepare the way . . .

Elizabeth: It doesn't sound to me as if his own way will be easy, does it, Zechariah?

Zechariah: The way of the chosen ones has never been easy, but they are the Lord's beloved.

Elizabeth: Not a light burden for a mother, but I bear it gratefully.

Zechariah: This is why you were chosen by the Lord, Elizabeth.

The two together: Blessed be the Name of the Lord.

(Pause)

Elizabeth: But, Zechariah, who is the one who will come after him? Whose way will our John prepare?

Zechariah: *(thoughtfully)* Remember the words that came to your lips when Mary came to visit us?

Elizabeth: *(quoting)* "Blessed are you among women and blessed is the fruit of your womb. And why has this happened to me, that the mother of my Lord comes to me?" *(a long pause. When she continues, she is deeply moved.)* Ah, Zechariah, it is Mary's son, Mary's son. *(Pause)*

Together: Come, Holy One, Come.

THE CAROLS

Anthems
"Riu, riu chiu," 16th c. Spanish
"The Angel Gabriel," Basque Carol

Hymns
"The Song of Zechariah," *The Hymnal 1982,* #S248–S252 (chant)
"The Song of Zechariah," *Wonder, Love, and Praise,* #889, #890
"Come and seek the ways of wisdom," *Voices Found,* #60
"Mary, when the angel's voice," *Voices Found ,* #64

A MEDITATION ON ELIZABETH AND ZECHARIAH

"And why has this happened to me,
that the mother of my Lord comes to me?"

(Luke 1:43)

I admit to a deep affection for the character of
Elizabeth, John's mother, and even for her husband,
Zechariah. For some reason I have always seen them as
people of humor and an appealing earthiness.[17]

Elizabeth, together with Mary of Nazareth, has become an
iconic personality. One cannot think of or admire paintings
relating to the Annunciation without also being made aware
of the importance of the Visitation. The classic depiction is of
an older woman meeting a younger woman, their faces joyful,
the bodies bending toward each other; yet, because most of
the art has them looking like medieval European women, the
pictures never touched me with their reality. It was the biblical story that did it. The one phrase that stays with me from
Luke's beautiful story as told in the Greek brings the visitation to mind vividly, thrills my imagination, and takes flesh
for me. I see the two women, and the story comes alive. Luke
1:41 in English says, "The baby leaped in her [Elizabeth's]

womb at her [Mary's] approach." But the original Greek has a wonderful verb *eskirtiseh*, which means a kind of trembling all over, as one does when goose bumps break out from joy, fear, or the approach of the divine. It is something like the ecstatic dancing of the Shakers in early American religion. I love the use of that verb so much—I don't think it is found elsewhere in Scriptures; while the Greek for *to leap* appears elsewhere in Scripture, the appearance of *eskirtiseh* is unique. This response of the baby may seem strange until we remember what the angel Gabriel said about John: "[e]ven before his birth he will be filled with the Holy Spirit."

That wonderful verb *eskirtiseh* stays in my mind with all its excitement and all its implications for John's later life and the awareness of his own mother's recognition of what is happening.

Elizabeth's story in a sense is the story of many childless women in the Bible. The first who comes to mind is Sarah (please see part 2 for more on Sarah) and then Hannah, Samuel's mother. It was considered a disfavor from God for a woman not to have children, especially boys. And, at a time when it was not known who or what determines the gender of the embryo, the *woman* was blamed for the condition of barrenness. It is a great tragedy that in places like India, even in our enlightened day, women are punished for the lack of male offspring, at times even by death, and the female children are aborted with a horrible frequency. We think that we have progressed astonishingly, but in human justice issues, much of humanity lags behind.

So Elizabeth was disgraced by her condition and considered it God's disfavor. Yet, she is not a bitter woman. Both of John's parents were reputed to be blameless before the Lord, a couple who lived according to the laws of their God, which was expected from people who were descendants of Aaron. When the angel Gabriel tells Zechariah that his wife will conceive, Zechariah insists that they are both too old. Again, we should take this according to the attitude of the times. Once a woman stopped the regular cycle of menses she was considered "too old," even though she may have been in her early forties. So don't imagine Elizabeth as an old woman. Yet, she obviously was much older than her cousin Mary. (*Cousin* used to cover many kinds of blood relationships.) All these are details. What is remarkable about Elizabeth is her utter selflessness, which we see clearly at the time of the Visitation.

She is enough of a woman of the times to be hiding during her pregnancy, but in the sixth month something remarkable happens. Her cousin from Nazareth arrives for a visit; which in itself is surprising: a young girl, in her early months of pregnancy, walking all the way from hilly Nazareth, south to the hills of Judea! One wonders which caravan she joined in order to get there; she could not have traveled that distance by herself. We are not sure exactly where Elizabeth and Zechariah lived in the Judean hills, but Luke tells us that Mary stayed with the couple for about three months.

I have often imagined the two women together. I have seen them so clearly in my imagination that I consider them friends and comforters in my hours of loneliness. Every expectant mother can imagine what their conversations were like, and how they phrased their dreams for their sons. In just a few words, what a lovely picture Luke has left us!

It is the initial greeting, however, that holds my attention. Elizabeth is the older of the two, with the assumed and accepted traditional superiority over the younger woman demanded by first-century custom. Yet, it's Elizabeth who proclaims astonishment and gratitude that the younger woman has come to visit. "And why has this happened to me, that the mother of my Lord comes to me?" Elizabeth's humility and the presence of the Holy Spirit in her, according to Luke's testimony, reveal to her that the younger woman's son will be superior to her own, but she doesn't flinch from this revelation. How much recognition, humility, and acceptance is included in that one verse—and how much this remarkable woman is able to teach us across the centuries.

Disregarding her own extraordinary experience, Elizabeth gives credit to Mary for her obedience to the Lord: "And blessed is she who believed that there would be a fulfillment of what was spoken to her by the Lord." What more can one say? Elizabeth is an inspiration and a credit to her gender. I love her.

A SPIRITUAL EXERCISE FOR WOMEN

Think of an older woman who has been a mentor to you. Write her a letter or, if this is no longer possible, write a prayer of thanks in her memory.

A SPIRITUAL EXERCISE FOR MEN

Think of a woman who has taught you about faith and trust (as Elizabeth taught her husband Zechariah) and tell the woman how important this has been in your life; if this is not possible, offer thanks to God for this particular woman of faith in your life.

LESSON 8

❈

Mary of Nazareth

The first paragraph is spoken with awe, as in a trance.

My eyes are blinded by light. I know that the Blessed Gabriel has left the room, for the brightness is not quite as intense as it has been. Still my eyes burn and everything inside me trembles. My soul has been seared by light. I must think on every word uttered. I will never forget any of them.

(Pause. Now she is telling the story)

My parents had gone to the fields to work, but I stayed behind to do the household chores, and afterward I withdrew for my prayers, as is my habit. I was reciting the hymn of Hannah, rejoicing in her words:

He raises up the poor from the
dust;

He lifts the needy from the ash
heap,
to make them sit with princes
and inherit a seat of honor. . . .

Suddenly a powerful presence entered the room. This is the only way I can describe it: it was like a moving light and a voice that sounded like the shofar, at times like the trumpet, combined with the sweetness of a lyre. I fell on my knees and could not stop trembling, but he said, "Greetings, you who are filled with grace. The Lord is with you." His words covered me with a peace I had not known before, as questions rushed to my mind. *What sort of greeting is this? What does it mean?* Despite the overwhelming sense of peace, I must have looked troubled for he said, "Do not be afraid, Mary, for you have found favor with God." I was covered with an awe that touched every part of my being when he proceeded to make me a promise reserved not for the lowly, like me, but for the great, like the princes of this earth. I do not dare utter it because it is the promise of a son, my son, whom I am to call Jesus, savior. Gabriel called him the Son of the Most High and reminded me that his ancestor was King David.

I did not at that moment stop to think of such astounding royal promises because there was another more urgent question. "How can this be? I know no man."

"The Holy Spirit will come upon you," he explained, "and the power of the Most High will overshadow you; therefore the child to be born will be holy; he will be called Son of God."

And while I was repeating the words, "the child to be born will be holy," he finished by saying, "Nothing will be impossible with God."

So I bowed my head and said, "Here I am, the servant of the Lord; let it be with me according to your word." These words of mine must have been enough for Gabriel, for he departed, leaving me bathed in his light.

I remain on my knees. I hold on to the light of his presence. I meditate on his words. If I let go I may be filled with fear again. I will *not* let go. I will repeat these words unendingly for the next nine months: "And now you will conceive in your womb and bear a son, and you will name him Jesus."

Jesus, I repeat, my son, Jesus. I start trembling again, but the promise comes to me like an echo filled with music, with the sweetness of a heavenly lyre: "The child to be born will be holy; he will be called Son of God."

I am filled with joy. Come, Holy Child, come!

THE CAROLS

Anthems
"The Mary Canticle," Leon Roberts (GIA Publications)

"Mary had a baby," arr. William Dawson (Tuskegee University Press)

"Mary was the Queen of Galilee," Wendall Whalum (Lawson-Gould)

Hymns
"Eternity touched hands with time," *Voices Found,* #39

"The Song of Mary," *The Hymnal 1982,* #S242–S247

"Magnificat," *HymnTune Psalter: Volume 1*, pp. 4, 36, 37, 69

"Magnificat," *Portland Psalter: Book 1*, p. 103

"My heart sings out with joyful praise," *My Heart Sings Out* , #60

A MEDITATION ON MARY'S GRACE

But she was much perplexed by his word and pondered
what sort of greeting this might be."

(Luke 1:29)

What is there left to say about Mary of Nazareth? I think she
herself would be surprised, even appalled, at much that has
been said and written about her. I am sure that she would be
offended by the worship that is directed toward her in many
parts of the world. There are extremes in people's view of the
mother of Jesus, just as there are extremes in the ways believers and agnostics view her son. It is difficult for Protestants
to understand the veneration of Mary by Roman Catholics
and Greek Orthodox, and it is equally difficult for the adher-
ents of those traditions to understand the near indifference of
many denominations to the person of Mary. The Greeks refer
to her as *Panayia*—the all holy. Even in the streets of Greece,
one hears spontaneous pleading addressed to her. Common
expressions, both sacred and profane—yes, even obscene—
reveal much of how a culture treats its saints.

Mary would probably have been horrified to think that
there might be statues of her in Catholic churches, or icons
honoring her in Byzantine sacred places. But whatever

Christians of various traditions think about the veneration of the mother of Jesus, this much is true: her obedience, her grace, her devotion, her purity, her immense sorrow, her love have all attracted worshipers through many centuries, and her person captures even the imagination of non-believers.

I have given voice to Mary in my monologues repeatedly; I cannot escape her. I have come to love her and ache for her as a mother. I cherish her devotion to her God as a young girl. And I marvel at her readiness to say Yes to God. But I was brought up as a strict Protestant and my coming to her appreciation was late. Yet, I consider my books as gifts from her because hers were the first monologues I wrote. That tells me something important. I have changed radically toward my view of Mary. That also tells me much about her.

There is no veneration of Mary found in any of the New Testament books, and only Matthew and Luke mention the virgin birth, and the legends about her started in the second century and much later, with Protoevangelion, the First Gospel of James. It is this writer, not the authors of the canonical books, who names Joachim and Anna as her parents. Their names may well be fact, but the rest of those stories are more magical than true.

But for me, it is the *humanity* of Mary that elevates her, not supernatural attributes. Jesus, as "born of a woman," is a powerful statement of the Incarnation.

As Jesus takes on a weighted meaning for the Christian, one that reflects the person's understanding of the Gospels' Jesus, so Mary means something personal to each one of us who meditates on her and her grace. As with her son, we cannot remain indifferent to her. Feelings for the mother of Jesus are tender—some strong, others fragile—and I feel compelled to cherish and respect them.

A SPIRITUAL EXERCISE

Who is Mary of Nazareth to you? Whatever your religious formation has been, take time now to think about her, to meditate on her person and on her willingness to say Yes to God. Then study the Passion passages. As you read about the grief of Mary, see the grief of mothers around the world who have lost sons to violence and war. Pray for healing and peace.

LESSON 9

⁂

Shepherds Abiding

The person reading the role of the shepherd would be quite believable with a beard or at least without a recent shave. A cape (not a fancy one but something that resembles a rough blanket) would add to the character. If the shepherd can speak in an unrefined accent that would be just right.

Nothing is lonelier than being a shepherd. We move with the flocks during the day, over rocky fields that yield scarce food for them, so we climb higher and higher, trying to find a richer pasture. During the night we huddle down with only the sheep for company. What we do is necessary; it is possible that people here in Palestine would starve without the meat and milk our sheep provide. Not that we get to sample much of it. Meat is reserved for those who have the money to buy it. You'd think that since we provide a necessary service, those who benefit from it would treat us like brothers. You would be wrong. Whenever we venture down-hill toward the towns and cities, we are shunned. We smell like sheep and goat, they tell us. And they stay away. Though necessary, we are unwanted and oftentimes invisible.

Why am I telling you all this? Ah, just listen and you will find out the wonderful thing that came to pass. And *we* were the ones so blessed, not the rich and powerful. We, the shepherds.

The night was clear and cold, as most nights are up here. We were gathered together in a group after a very tiring day of climbing to new pastures. The fire embers were dying and we were trying to make ourselves comfortable under the sheep-skins that serve as our blankets. Most of us press the shep-herd's crook into the soil, hang the furry cloak from it so as to make a little tent, to protect us from the night dew, and then try to sleep on the hard ground. But that night none of us seemed ready to sleep. We had a storyteller among us and we were listening to his voice retelling the story of the promised Messiah. "The prophets foretold. . . ," he said again, trying to put some energy in the telling, to give us some of the hope that had been robbed from us during the years under the Roman yoke. Abruptly, the storyteller stopped. He looked up and we did the same. Something stirred in the skies, some-thing that seemed so close we could touch it—a bright, silver movement, like the shooting stars we were so used to seeing, but much closer, much brighter. "Ah!!!" we all cried and tried to shield our eyes, but a voice we did not recognize stopped us. "Do not be afraid," it said, and we immediately calmed down and listened. Songs were filling the bright, shining air around us. Holding our breath, many of us on our knees from the awe that covered us, we listened. "Glory to God on high," the voices sang. "Good news to all people," they told us—us, the shepherds. "Peace on earth."

And they led us to a child in a manger. We were the only honored guests. We, the poor shepherds. Glory to God on high, and peace to all on earth.

THE CAROLS

Anthems

"A Shepherd's Carol," Benjamin Britten (Oxford University Press)

"He shall feed his flock," from *Messiah* by G. F. Handel

"What is this lovely fragrance," Gerald Near

Hymns

"Break forth, O beauteous heavenly light," *The Hymnal 1982,* #91

"Go, tell it on the mountain," *The Hymnal 1982,* #99

"Go, tell it on the mountain," *Lift Every Voice and Sing,* #21

A MEDITATION ON THE GOOD SHEPHERD

——————————————— ❀ ———————————————

The Lord is my shepherd, I shall not want.
He makes me lie down in green pastures;
he leads me beside still waters;
he restores my soul.

(Psalm 23:1–3)

——————————————— ❀ ———————————————

The metaphor of the shepherd is one of the most frequently encountered in the biblical story. The word *sheep* (together with rams and lambs) is found in at least five hundred references. This is a predominant, lively, and tender image in both Testaments. Sheep appear very early in the history of humanity, as early as Genesis. Where there are sheep, of course, there are always shepherds. It is remarkable that God refers to the Godself as a shepherd. Shepherding certainly was not an exalted occupation in ancient times, but, even so, it was frequently coupled in the Old Testament with the most exalted of human titles: The *king* of Israel is also called the *shepherd* of Israel.

The references are unmistakable. It is apparent at the very beginning of the monarchy that God expects Saul to be a shepherd-king: both a servant and a king. When Saul fails and God sends Samuel to find Saul's successor among the sons of Jesse, David is not present because he is tending the family's sheep.

Some shepherd images have entered the language and imagery of those who have grown up in the Jewish and Christian faiths, images that have remained in the collective subconscious to be called up in times of distress or need. "The Lord is my shepherd; I shall not want . . . thy rod and thy staff, they comfort me . . ." are among the most loved and recognized words in all of Scripture. And the beautiful poem of Second Isaiah made glorious and unforgettable in the music of Handel's *Messiah*:

> He shall feed his flock like a shepherd,
> he will gather the lambs in his arms,
> he will carry them in his bosom,
> and gently lead those that are with young.
>
> (Isaiah 40:11)

The most thoroughly developed image of the shepherd in the Old Testament is found in Ezekiel 34. The speaker is the Lord and his wrath and bitter hurt are directed toward the unfaithful shepherds of Israel—the failed kings. "Ah, you shepherds of Israel who have been feeding yourselves!" he exclaims (v. 2), and then he continues with a litany of what these shepherds have left undone:

> "You have not strengthened the weak,
> you have not healed the sick,
> you have not bound up the injured,
> you have not brought back the strayed,
> you have not sought the lost. . . ." (v. 4)

Then the Lord God takes the role of shepherd for himself. "I myself will be the shepherd of my sheep" (v. 15a) and all that the false shepherds have failed to do the Good Shepherd will do. It is no wonder that the church saw this as the messianic promise fulfilled in Jesus.

The metaphor of the shepherd appears in the New Testament, too, with even greater tenderness and intimacy. Jesus, in John 10, calls himself both the shepherd and the gate through which the sheep enter the fold. A man of the country who no doubt had observed shepherds and their sheep, Jesus tells of the sheep that recognize the voice of the shepherd and follow only him. Then he goes far beyond the familiar image found in the Old Testament's understanding of the shepherd's role, proclaiming: "I am the good shepherd. *The good shepherd lays downs his life for the sheep.*" Five times, in the span of six verses, Jesus repeats this: "I lay down my life," foretelling of the coming sacrifice. Jesus goes beyond the prophets, who had seen Yahweh as the good shepherd but not as the One who dies for the flock.

And here lies the glory of the *covenant of peace* that Yahweh makes anew in Ezekiel's prophecy and Jesus fulfills in his own person: the shepherd who gives his life for his sheep. This is the wondrous fulfillment of the ancient promise: "My sheep hear my voice. I know them, and they follow me. I give them eternal life, and they will never perish. No one will snatch them out of my hand. What my father has given me is greater than all else, and no one can snatch it out of the Father's hand. The Father and I are one" (John 10:27–30).

Oh Shepherd of the heart, the soul, and the mind.
Stay with us through the dark. Lead us home.
     We are lost,
frightened and weary. We listen to strange voices and,
confused because of our disobedience,
we follow those to whom we don't belong.
The seduction of possessions and the clamor of false tunes
lead us astray. Let us hear your voice;
let us recognize it and follow it.
Lead us back to the fold, oh Christ, back
to your protective arms.[18]

A Spiritual Exercise

There are many voices clamoring for our attention today. My students seem to have attachments to their ears—cell phones, iPods—and they are not the only ones. "Whose voice are you listening to?" I want to ask. "Whom are you following?" And this is the question all of us need to answer: Whose is the voice that calls us? What voice do we recognize as belonging to our Shepherd, to the One who loves us and knows us and calls us by name? Take time during Advent to think on these questions and to answer them.

Part II

Voices Crying in the Wilderness

Introduction

The land is not able to bear all [their] words.

(Amos 7:10c)

The secularizing of the Christmas season with increasing emphasis on things and glitter, with the false gaiety and occasional obscenity of office parties, and with the *ad nauseum* use in the marketplace of precious and delightful Christmas carols—all these distractions threaten to obliterate the sacred meaning, to prevent meditation, and to discourage thoughtfulness in this season. The church at large has not helped by starting decorations, performances, and the singing of carols during the season of Advent rather than waiting for Christmastide. The liturgical churches (Episcopal, Roman Catholic, Lutheran, and many Methodist), to their credit, have struggled valiantly to preserve the solemnity and meaning of Advent as a time of preparation and repentance by adhering to the Scripture readings for Advent and by waiting until Christmas Eve for the carols and decorations.

In the early centuries of Christianity, Advent was similar to Lent in its emphasis on penitence and fasting, while in recent years there has been an increasing emphasis on celebration, hope, and anticipation. Yet the lectionary readings for Advent are filled with calls for repentance, with themes of darkness that leads eventually to light, with the prophetic voices of the past, with our yearnings of the present time as we participate in our liturgy and practice faithfulness, and with our hopes for the future and our expectation of Jesus' Second Coming.

In this portion of the book, we'll open our hearts to these prophetic voices from the past and listen carefully to all these Advent themes. We'll pay close attention to the words and promises of the prophets and tap into their awareness of God's salvation in the present and the future. We'll look briefly at the apocalyptic undercurrent of Advent: its focus on the "last things," the end of time, a recurring theme in many Advent readings. We'll enter into the Advent movement from expectation to fulfillment, as we read the words of those who recognized that God's saving event had finally arrived.

In the meditations that follow, these voices will speak to us again. The speakers are people of the promise and prophets whose words resonate throughout the season, mostly ignored by those who read them or listen to them, and utterly disregarded by the world at large. You might want to use this portion of the book for private meditation so that Advent will become more meaningful. You might also use these meditations for public readings, followed by small group discussion during the Christian formation sessions, or even for a special Advent liturgy. The monologues in part II are also appropriate for other seasons in the church calendar year. The readings and discussions can be used over the course of at least six Sundays, with enough left over for private meditation. My special hope is that young people will find an opportunity to use these offerings as drama. There is no more exciting study than that of the biblical stories. Drama makes them come alive, and young people are attracted to life and to drama.

✤ Words of Promise

Let us listen to the first words of promise.

As long as the earth endures
seedtime and harvest, cold
and heat
summer and winter,
day and night,
shall not cease.

(Genesis 8:22)

"Go from your country and your kindred and your
father's house to the land that I will show you. I will
make of you a great nation, and I will bless you, and
make your name great, so that you will be a blessing. I

will bless those who bless you and the one who curses you I will curse and in you all the families of the earth shall be blessed."

(Genesis 12:1a–3)

"I will surely return to you in due season and your wife Sarah shall have a son."

(Genesis 18:10)

"What troubles you, Hagar? Do not be afraid; for God has heard the voice of the boy where he is. Come, lift up the boy and hold him fast with your hand, for I will make a great nation of him."

(Genesis 21:17b–18)

SARAH:
THE ANCESTOR OF THE PROMISE

Is anything too wonderful for the Lord?
At the set time I will
return to you, in due season,
and Sarah shall have a son.

(Genesis 18:14)

Cluck-cluck, chatter-chatter, wail and weep. I am tired of it all. Stop it!

You must remain quiet in order to listen to me. There's not much breath left in me—look how old I've become. I'm about to disappear. Take care to hear me, since there's no woman left to tell you the truth after I'm gone. The men will try, but they will ignore you in the telling; they will share it only with men, and men tell stories differently from us. So stop your wailing and pay attention.

You can't even guess at it now—and no one except Abraham is living who remembers—but once I was very beautiful. So beautiful that he had to hide me from other men and, worse, at crucial times, he had to lie about me. But I'll come to that later. The first thing you need to know is that *God included me in the promise.* Did you hear me clearly? God included me in the promise. He told Abraham that he would make him the ancestor of a great nation, that his descendants would be countless like the stars (you know how we love to exaggerate here in the desert!). But there was no way the promise would be fulfilled without me. I was his wife, and only I could be the mother of the son who would be the fulfillment of the promise. Are you following me?

Yes, I see that you are. You have wiped your tears, and you are quiet. I cannot see you well, but I can guess, I can guess. I have known women for so long. Some of you are really interested, others are already thinking of how to prove me false, some are wondering how you will take advantage of my words, and then others are already planning how to change my story in the retelling. But it's enough that one or two of you understand.

When God made the promise to Abraham, my husband believed him. He didn't say anything—that was his way—but he believed everything Yahweh told him, and for most of our life together he acted on that belief: that Yahweh loved him and would make him the ancestor of a great nation. But it's not always easy to live on promises.

When the great famine came, Abram, as he was called then, took all of us with him and started on the long, long trek to Egypt. Up to then I had loved and cherished and obeyed him. I was glad he thought enough of me to take me away from a land suffering famine. But when we reached the borders of Egypt and started smelling the waters of the Nile, he came to me and took me aside, away from the always-prying eyes and listening ears of our servants and relatives. "Sarai," he said— for that was my name then—"Sarai, you are very beautiful. Because of your beauty, when the Egyptians see you, my life will be in great danger. They will let *you* live, but in order to take you from me, they will kill me. Will you save my life? Tell them you are my sister; they will spare your brother but not your husband." I was astounded. This was the man Yahweh had chosen as the founder of a great nation? A man who lied about his wife? A man who feared for his life? And for the first time I thought, *If he trusts in God's promise, why did he leave the land chosen for him by God? And if he trusts in God's promise, how can he put in danger the one who is able to fulfill this promise?* Of course, being a young wife, I could not let him know my thoughts, so I told him I would save his life.

We were stopped at the border, as was the custom, to ask permission to enter the city where Pharaoh dwelt, and before I knew it I was taken away from Abram. You see, we had to uncover our faces, to be examined, strangers that we were, and the gossip about my looks reached even the king's ears. Abram did what I had expected. He introduced me as his sister, Sarai, and I said not a word. Within the same day a man from the palace came riding on a horse and before I could say goodbye to Abram he had ridden away with me to the palace.

There, I entered another world. The palace was very beautiful, but everything was strange beyond my imagining, the women hostile, the children unhappy, and I, alone and trembling in my elegant bedroom. Soon slaves surrounded me bathing me and dressing me in the Egyptians' fine but immodest attire, so different from my rough desert clothing, fussing with my hair, even coloring my eyes and lips. And I could say nothing. That night, Pharaoh came to me and made me his wife. My anger knew no bounds. How could I be two men's wife? I knew that men like Abram could take their slaves to their bed or even choose more than one wife, but he had promised that I would be his only wife. Now here I was with everything I had known turned upside down. All I could do was pray to Yahweh to punish the men who abused me and to keep me from having a child with this stranger.

I don't know how many days I stayed there. I heard rumors that Abram was now a rich man because Pharaoh was so pleased with the beauty of his sister! I refused to speak to anyone except for my prayers to Yahweh. And I thought they were being answered, because soon, Pharaoh's visits to me became less frequent, until he called me to his presence, something unheard of during the day. In the light of day he looked old and sick and everyone around him seemed to be weeping.

He said, "Sarai, have I not been good to you?"

I decided to answer him; I said, "I have no complaints."

"But how can that be?" he persisted. "Since you came into my household, nothing but sorrow has entered with you. What have I done to offend your gods?"

"It is Yahweh you have offended, your majesty," I said, sick of the lies and almost sorry for him. "I am Abram's *wife*, not his sister."

Then Pharaoh tore at his robe and cried for Abram to be brought before him. Abram entered unperturbed, but when he saw me in my royal finery, he flinched. I stood there, staring at him, while Pharaoh, the great king, pleaded with my husband. "What have you done to me?" he asked. "Why did you tell me she was your sister? Your god has punished me because of your lie. Take her, take her and all that I have given you and leave my land!"

And so, under military escort, we departed from Egypt and I was no longer one of Pharaoh's queens.

I was not happy with Abram either. Maybe this is the reason I stayed barren for so long. The promise was still there, but it kept being endangered because *I* was in danger. Do you understand? I longed for a child. As the years passed, I lost patience, and I made the terrible mistake of giving my maid, Hagar, to my husband so he could have a child with her; the child would be mine by law. But instead of humility, Hagar showed arrogance and I punished her by telling Abram to get rid of her. How she managed to survive and return is her story and I don't care to remember it.

I want to come back to Yahweh's promise. My beauty had already gone, my years had grown long, and there I was, still barren, with Abraham acting as always—trusting in his God. I had given up. I had forgotten the promise, since there was no possibility of fulfillment. Three times God had saved me from extreme danger, and three times I thought, *Now the promise will be fulfilled; this is why my life was spared.* But nothing happened until that day when the three strange men approached our tent.

How beautiful they were, as if the desert sun had not touched them, clean and shiny, dressed in brilliant white. Abraham, hospitable always, invited them to eat. I was hiding behind the flap of the tent, listening, for when Abraham went into negotiations, I became suspicious. But soon I was pleased to be asked to bake for them while Abraham gave orders for the roasting of the calf. As they were eating, I heard a voice ask Abraham, "Where is Sarah, your wife?" He told them I was in the tent, but instead of calling me out I heard one of them say the strangest words: "I will surely return to you in the spring and Sarah your wife shall have a son." I laughed. What else could I have done? And they heard me. "Why did she laugh?" they asked my husband. "Is anything too difficult for the Lord?" and then I was afraid. Who were these men? Who had sent them? So I lied; "I didn't laugh," I said, but their fierce countenances turned to the tent; they saw through it, they saw through me, and I was afraid I had destroyed all hope for us.

But I was not punished. I was, after all, the one through whom the promise would be fulfilled, no matter my unbelief, no matter my laughter. With the spring, Isaac was born and the rest is known to you. Now bring my son to me, and let me tell him what only his ears must hear.

Thinking about Sarah

Though there are many references to Sarah in the Abraham sagas, we do not really know her. We hear about her from others: from the narrators and from Hagar. It is not a flattering portrait, but there is much also that can be said in her defense.

FOR REFLECTION

- Put yourself in Sarah's place. What does it mean to be given a promise that you believe with all your heart is from God—but that doesn't seem to be fulfilled? What would you do to help bring it about?

- Put yourself in her place when Isaac returned from that almost fatal journey with his father: "Mother, mother, my father almost killed me today but the Lord saved me!" As a mother, how would you respond?

- What is the meaning of jealousy? Think of the many women who are put aside today in favor of other, younger versions of themselves, with no one lifting a voice in their defense. What does it mean to be discarded by the one who has vowed to cherish you? Though Sarah held her ground, what was the cost?

HAGAR:
A PARALLEL PROMISE

"Have I really seen God and remained
alive after seeing him?"

(Genesis 16:13b)

Sarai, my mistress, thinks I am dumb. Otherwise she would
never have chosen me to give to Abram the child she could
not give him. Sarai wanted me to be invisible and silent.
When I fooled her, she exploded.

They had brought me to their household from Egypt
when I was just a girl, my face still beautiful and my body
strong, my mind quick and alert at all times. I listened and I
learned. Abram, her husband, was a quiet man, given to long
hours of sitting alone on the sand, his eyes closed against the
fierce sun, his neck and head straight as if he was listening.

Sarai was a good mistress, most of the time. She too was
beautiful, but sad. At first, I had no suspicion of her mean-
ness. I helped her dress in the mornings, I prepared her meals
when she was alone, and I taught her some of the secrets of
my Egyptian tribe—how to look her best when her husband
came to her. And then I disappeared from her presence, for
this was my fate as her maid. But my ears never shut and my
eyes saw everything around me.

I had just come into full womanhood when I noticed
Sarai looking at me as if she saw me. I would feel her eyes following me when I left her tent to go to my other chores. She
had become increasingly nervous and her sadness had begun
to rob her face of beauty. Sometimes I caught her crying and

complaining to her god that he had shown no favor to her because she was without child. I heard both husband and wife talking about Yahweh as if they knew him personally.

On a day when she seemed more nervous than before, Sarai sent orders for me to wash myself properly at the well and to put on my finer dress, the one she had given me when I came of age. She looked both sad and excited, the way women look when they are waiting for something that may prove to be good or bad. She said to Abram in my hearing: "The Lord has prevented me from having children; take the maid as your wife and maybe I will have children by her." I knew this was accepted in their part of the world, but I wanted her to call me by name, to say "Hagar," to make me feel that I was a woman like her now that we would share a husband. But she never did; she never gave me my name. Abram was not much better. He seemed pleased to have me near him at night, but he never talked to me. He was a silent man, afraid of his wife.

When I knew that I was with child I longed desperately to talk with another woman—I who had never known a mother—but the slaves stayed away from me now that I was Abram's wife, and Sarai looked at me with hostility, even though it was her decision that I be given to Abram.

When I felt the child stir in my womb I said aloud to Abram: "Now, finally, you will have a son." He said not a word, but I heard a hiss behind me and turned to find Sarai looking at me as if she would kill me. It made me feel very angry and very foolish. "Look," I said to her, throwing my proud Egyptian hair back and lifting up my head. "Look, the child you wanted is growing inside *me*!"

She said to Abram, "Husband, I must speak to you," and Abram, as was his habit, followed her to her own tent. I don't know what she said to him, but I soon found out. He did not come to me at night, and Sarai made every effort to show me that she hated me. She seemed to be following me around, making sure that all the heavy work fell on me, and nothing I did pleased her. I tried to avoid her, to become invisible again for the sake of the child growing in me, but she heaped abuse on me and my unborn baby. One day, I heard her ordering the head slave to whip me, for no reason at all that I could see, except that I was still alive, still healthy, the child moving in my belly. When I heard her speaking to the head slave, I ran away.

I moved south, away from the tents and the sheep of Abram's oasis, not knowing where I was going, only sensing that I needed to be far from Sarai's anger. I hoped, though I knew little about the direction that would take me there, that I was making my way toward Egypt. It was the middle of the day when I left and I walked until nightfall, trying to stay near some vegetation, so that I could find water. I slept in the wilderness that night, shivering in the cold, suspecting that if I didn't find a group of people soon who would be willing to help me I would die, along with the child in my womb.

It was the thought of the child that kept me alert and in the morning moved me toward a spring of water. I bent to drink and I heard a voice. "Hagar, where are you coming from and where are you going?" I was stunned to be called by name. Without lifting up my head, afraid of whom I would see, I answered, "I am running away from the face of Sarai, my mistress."

The voice said, "Return to her, Hagar, and submit to her." I then lifted my head, ready to protest, to cry out at the injustice, but the sight stopped me, and I remained with my mouth open, no sound escaping. What I saw cannot be described, so I will not try. I said to myself, "It is the angel of the Lord. Pay attention." But when the voice continued, I knew the Presence was more than that. "Are you the Yahweh they are talking about all the time?" I wanted to ask, but I didn't. The One who saw me in my distress then continued with the words I would teach my son and he would teach his children, and in turn they would remember them for generations to come:

> Now you have conceived and
> shall bear a son;
> you shall call him Ishmael,
> for the LORD has given heed to
> your affliction.
> He shall be a wild ass of a man,
> with his hand against everyone,
> and everyone's hand against
> him.

The promise was unmistakable: "Hagar, I will multiply your offspring into multitudes."

I fell prostrate before the Lord. With my face to the ground I raised my voice and cried, "You are the seeing God!" and I waited to die because this Lord had allowed me to see him. Time passed; all was quiet. No voice, no movement, and no death for me—not yet. "Is it possible that I have seen the

Lord and remained alive after seeing him?" I cried, but there was no one there to answer.

I lifted myself up, shook the dust off my clothes, touched the child in my belly, and I started to say, "Ha, I bet Sarai has not seen the Lord and lived," but something powerful stopped me: the echo of a voice saying, "Return to your mistress and submit to her," and the echo of a promise.

"Behave, Hagar," I told myself all the way back to the tents of Abram. "For the sake of the child, for the sake of the One who spoke to you, a humble girl, behave before Sarai, no matter what the cost. You heard a promise, and the promise of this God must be fulfilled."

I did exactly as the Lord told me to do and the child was born healthy and wild, as promised. He was never sick and never afraid of anything or anyone. I trembled for him, but he jumped into and out of danger unscathed. We were happy for a while. Even Sarai tolerated us. And then, against all that seems to make sense under heaven, she too bore Abraham a son. They did look rather ridiculous at their age, but the child was sweet and my Ishmael loved him. Sarah finally was filled with laughter. I watched her from afar and saw a happy woman. I had not forgotten her earlier abuse of me, but all seemed to go well for Ishmael and me, because Abraham loved both his sons.

Two years later, when Isaac was weaned, Abraham gave a great celebration, a feast for all—something he had not done for Ishmael—but we both were there for Isaac's happy day. My Ishmael, rambunctious as always, was running around and letting Isaac, on his short legs, try to follow him and catch him. As I watched them, Ishmael slowed down to let the little one come close and then turned suddenly and grabbed Isaac in a big hug. The boys laughed together and Isaac put his thin arms around his brother's strong neck and hugged him tightly. I felt such pride; my son with *her* son. But then my blood chilled because I noticed that her eyes too had followed the movement of the boys. And then I saw her severe gaze fall on Abraham.

I grabbed Ishmael and ran to my tent with him, for I knew something bad was coming. The next morning it arrived in the person of a sad, silent Abraham. He handed me a sack with bread and a skin of water, lifted Ishmael for a last embrace and a kiss, put him on my back and, hiding his cowardly face from the child, he left the tent. We were exiled.

At first Ishmael thought it was a game we were playing, running away and hiding. But the desert was burning and even he, after a while, felt the heat and asked for water. I trembled at the thought of what would happen when the skin I held ran dry. How many hours, how many days passed? It's hard to tell, in the desert. Soon, there was not a drop of water left to drink and no bread to eat. Ishmael, who had stopped running, was silent. Now his strong little body seemed too heavy for his legs and he lifted up his arms for me to hold him. I picked him up as I always did when he wanted me to love him, and I struggled to keep on walking. The hours passed under a merciless sun, and I knew we would die that very day. The child's lips were dry and his breath was labored. The moment came when I knew I could no longer carry him. There was some brush in my path, but no water. I found a spot where shade would fall eventually, and I placed the child on the ground. He was dying, but I did not want to see it.

I walked away so I could no longer hear the pitiful crying escaping his lips—he who had never whined—and I thought bitterly about Yahweh's promises as I backed away from the child who was a promise.

I crouched down, watching the child from afar, not wanting to see his death but unable to take my eyes from him. I cried out with what little strength remained in my throat, I cried and wept without tears on and on until the sound must have reached the heavens. For there it was again, that voice I recognized. "What troubles you, Hagar?" *What troubles me? I wanted to scream but I couldn't. Can't you see my child is dying? You, who said he'd be blessed? What troubles me?*

I couldn't make a sound but the voice continued, "Do not be afraid, Hagar," and, surprising myself, I did stop being afraid. But then, when nothing happened, I thought, *I am dying, I'm dreaming all this. This is the end.*

The voice said, "God heard the voice of the boy where he is. Come, pick him up, hold him, he will live and be the father of a great nation."

I stood up and looked around me. I still thought I was dying, but then I heard a sound like the gurgling of water and saw the spring so close to me that I couldn't quite take it in. Why hadn't I heard it earlier? And what did he mean when he said that he had heard the voice of the boy instead of mine? There was no time to ask. This time there was no Presence, only a voice. I still held the skin in my hand and I bent down to fill it and to drink the water so that I would have the strength to lift the child. I ran to him and poured the water tenderly into his mouth letting the cool blessedness wash his brown, beloved skin.

We were saved. I would not return to Abraham and Sarah. We were finished with them and they were finished with us. But the God who had plans for my son stayed with us. *I* would be the ancestor of Ishmael's descendants, not Abraham. I would be the one who found him a wife from Egypt. The promises were for us also.

Thinking about Hagar

Biblical scholar Phyllis Trible places Hagar's story among *The Texts of Terror.* Each of the texts is introduced with a tombstone on which Trible ascribes words from the Suffering Servant of Second Isaiah.[19] Hagar's story is pertinent today in light of the tragedies that have resulted from our misunderstanding of her supposed descendants, the people of Islam. (But I think of Ishmael's true descendants as the Bedouins, the nomads who continue to live the kind of life he lived in the desert.)

Hagar is extremely important in Islamic tradition, and she is still highly revered by Muslims. Even Israelis who seek peace between themselves and Palestinians emphasize the connection of the displaced Palestinians to the expulsion of Hagar.

And consider these remarkable points: in the entire Bible, Hagar is the only woman who "sees Yahweh and lives." She is the only woman ancestor of a tribe, and she is the only woman who chooses a wife for her son. I had always felt a deep regret and sadness when I considered Hagar. I must have seen a drawing of her when I was a child, because the impact of it has never left me. In that drawing, Hagar is running, alone, her face turned toward those she has left behind. There is no regret on her face, only terror. It is the terror that stays with me. And, perhaps, something that I recognized much later as guilt. In my culture, I don't remember sensing compassion for "fallen women." Was Hagar one of them? Or was she one of the foreign, lost women we saw begging in the streets of European cities after World War II? Is Hagar one of the refugee women who continue to be abused throughout the world today? All these associations stayed with me but were finally exorcised when I wrote about Hagar, in her voice.

FOR REFLECTION

- What is your opinion of Hagar?

- Whom does she represent for you?

- What does her story tell us about justice? about the treatment of women? about slaves or servants?

Words That Urge Repentance: The Day of the Lord

Let us listen to the voices of the prophets.

Blow the trumpet in Zion;
sound the alarm on my holy
mountain!
Let all the inhabitants of the land
tremble.
For the day of the LORD is
coming, it is near—
a day of darkness and gloom,
a day of clouds and thick
darkness!

. . .

Truly the day of the LORD is great,
terrible indeed—who can
endure it?

(Joel 2:1, 11)

For the LORD of hosts has a day
against all that is proud and lofty,
against all that is lifted up and high. . . .
The haughtiness of people shall be humbled.
And the pride of everyone shall be brought low. . . .

(Isaiah 2:12, 17)

Wail, for the day of the Lord
Is near;
It will come like destruction from the Almighty!
See, the day of the Lord comes,
cruel, with wrath and fierce
anger,
to make the earth a desolation,
and to destroy its sinners from it.

(Isaiah 13:6, 9)

For the day of the LORD is near
against all the nations.
As you have done, it shall be done
to you;
your deeds shall return on your own head.

(Obadiah 1:15)

That day will be a day of wrath,
a day of distress and anguish,
a day of ruin and devastation,
a day of darkness and gloom,
a day of clouds and thick
darkness. . . .
Be silent before the Lord GOD!
For the day of the Lord is
at hand.

(Zephaniah 1:15, 7)

**The voices lead us to the prophet who gave a new meaning
to the Day of the Lord.**

AMOS:
A VOICE OF COURAGE

Alas, for those who are at ease in Zion

Alas for you who desire the day
of the Lord!
Why do you want the day of
the Lord?
It is darkness, not light;
is not the day of the Lord
darkness, not light,
and gloom with no brightness
in it?

(Amos 5:18–20)

I knew immediately it was the voice of the Lord. High up in the sycamore tree I was pinching the fruit so the rest would grow large for the poor to have something to eat. My mind was on the laborers of the land, my hands moving as if on their own, when the word of God first spoke to me and I tumbled down from the tree. I was a strong young man so my body didn't suffer. Only my mind was invaded. In stunned silence, like a sleepwalker, I moved to my evening work, the tending of sheep. With the voice of Yahweh passionate in my ears, I made my way to the fold to make sure they were safe and none were lost.

The voice persisted above the bleating of the lambs and the calling of the ewes. I stayed the night with them thinking on the God who made the Pleiades and Orion, who darkens the day into night. The dark was pierced by the lights of the stars as my soul was pierced by the call of Yahweh. I listened through the night to a drumbeat of words that filled me with grief.

Here in Tekoa where we live our quiet, difficult lives, we seem to be isolated, yet news reaches those of us who are interested in what the nations are doing to each other and how they behave before the Creator of the stars and of the earth. Travelers have brought me frightening news from Gaza; horrific images of evil from the Amorites, from Syria and Tyre and Edom. I was well familiar with the transgressions of the nations that surround us. That night I heard again of their evil against the helpless and listened to the promised punishments from the Lord.

They beat in my head: *"Thus says the Lord. For three transgressions and for four I will not revoke the punishment. . . ."* The rhythm of transgressions and the destruction to follow was in my ears, the visions etched before my eyes.

In the following days I prepared myself for a long journey in obedience to the voice of the Lord, who ordered me to Bethel and Samaria. On my shepherd's crook I hung a sack with bread and cheese and a skin filled with water. Inside the sack I also hid a plumb line. I placed the staff on my back, rested my elbows on the crooked wood, and walked north toward Jerusalem, stopping on the way to listen to poor people who were moving to or away from the city. They told me their sad stories: the rich were growing richer in the extreme these days, but the poor were getting poorer; there was hunger in the midst of plenty. "Prophets have become slaves of the governing powers," the travelers told me, "twisting the truth to match the words of those who hold power in their hands." I made mental notes of what I heard, painfully aware that instead of diminishing, the number of transgressions was rising, but these were the transgressions of Judah and Israel, not of foreign lands. The pain in my chest increased. The drumbeat continued: *"Thus says the Lord, for three transgressions and for four I will not revoke the punishment. . . says the Lord."*

I bypassed Jerusalem, but by the time I reached the gates of Bethel, where the king had set his sanctuary, I had heard enough. I saw the poor being pushed out of the gate, their scant harvest robbed from them, so the women of the rich could lie on ivory beds. I stood inside the wall near their idols—the altars of their moneymaking—and cried out:

Oh you who
trample on the poor
and take from them levies of grain,
you have built houses of hewn stone,
but you shall not live in them,
you have planted pleasant vineyards,
but you shall not drink their wine.
. . . you who afflict the righteous, who
take a bribe,
and push aside the needy in the gate.

I moved farther into the city and stood on a wall being built for one of the houses of the priests; the Lord ordered me to take out the plumb line that shook in my hand, for I had seen the vision of the Lord with the plumb line in his own hand, and the Lord had asked me, *Amos, what do you see?* Now the Lord spoke through me and I cried out, "Thus says the Lord: 'The sanctuaries of Israel shall be laid waste, and I will rise against the house of Jeroboam with the sword.'"

There was commotion all around me, people running away from me, some throwing stones, but others coming closer to listen, their clothes in rags, their faces gaunt from hunger. One of them asked me, "What about us, Amos? Has the Lord turned from us also? Is the Lord with us?" I felt compassion for them and said, "Seek good and not evil, that you may live; and so the Lord, the God of hosts, will be with you, just as you have said."

I kept walking into the city and saw the shops, the eagerness in the trading, the reluctance to slow down the buying and selling even on the Sabbath; I saw women being borne in carriages dripping with finery and I averted my eyes. Representatives of the prophetic guild approached me to argue with me: "Who are you to tell us of the Lord's words to us?" they demanded. "We are the ones who will be vindicated on the day of the Lord, for Israel shall triumph over all nations."

It was then that the anger of the Lord filled me like a fire and I saw it all happening before my eyes as I cried: "Alas for you who desire the day of the Lord! Why do you want the day of the Lord? It is darkness, not light; is not the day of the Lord darkness, not light, and gloom with no brightness in it?"

"Blasphemy, blasphemy," they screamed at me. "We are the Lord's chosen." The crowd parted as Amaziah, the court prophet, approached in all his finery, looking more like a peacock than a priest, to confront me. A ragged laborer climbed near me and whispered, "Amos, he will do you harm. He has already sent word to the king to tell him that you are conspiring against him. *The land cannot bear all Amos' words*, he said to Jeroboam." But I cried out loud enough for Amaziah to hear: "Jeroboam shall die by the sword, and Israel must go into exile away from his land."

Amaziah said, "O seer, go away, flee to the land of Judah and never again prophesy here where the king has set his sanctuary!"

"How can I?" I wondered aloud. "It is the Lord who plucked me from following the sheep and the Lord who told me, 'Go prophesy to my people Israel.'"

Amaziah then sent his servants against me and they pushed me outside the gate of Bethel. But before exiting I cried out,

"Hear this, you that trample on the needy, and bring to ruin the poor of the land. . .I will turn your feasts into mourning, and all your songs into lamentation."

A few of the friends I had made on the way stayed with me, and we trudged back toward Judah. We raised our voices and wept together. Then they asked, "Amos, what can we do?" and I called to the Lord, "O Lord God, cease, I beg you! How can Jacob stand? He is so small!" The Lord relented concerning this; "This also shall not be," said the Lord God.

Before returning to my flock and my sycamore trees, I said to my friends: "It may come to pass that you are the remnant of the Judah that the Lord will save. But remember, my people, "Let justice roll down like waters, and righteousness like an ever-flowing stream."

Thinking about Amos

Amos possessed a powerful, original mind, and a fearless heart and voice. He, like Isaiah, is startling in his universalism. Unlike many others in Israel and Judah, he proclaimed that God's care extended to all nations, not only to Israel; God's saving grace and blessing were available for everyone. For Amos, election, the conviction that God had chosen Israel for the fulfillment of God's promises to humankind, means greater responsibility, so he does not absolve Israel of guilt even though she is "chosen." He sees the day of the Lord equally as frightening for the Israelites as it will be for foreign nations, the Gentiles, and this is his original contribution to the meaning of the Day of the Lord. Amos did not originate this concept of the Day of Yahweh, but, like all prophets, he borrowed from the depth of the tradition of Jewish Scripture and testimony the belief in a God who involves himself in the history and the affairs of his people with his *word* and his *acts*. Amos's contemporaries thought of "the day of the Lord" as a day of deliverance and light for themselves alone—salvation for Israel. But Amos, filled with anguish at the Jews' easy living, luxury, immorality, and injustice, sees it as a day of darkness, disaster, and judgment. His anguish and incredulity are obvious.

The important message that jumps out at me and will not let me go is this: *Israel, especially up to the exile, believed she had God on her side.* At the time of Amos she was living in rare peace—the forty years of the reign of Jereboam II. During this time, Israel expanded her territory, her military was strong and successful, the economy was good, and the luxury of the rich was scandalous to a prophet like Amos. But Israel, encouraged by her official priests, was convinced that God was on her side. What can possibly sound more contemporary to our ears, in the prosperous West, at a time when so many of us are deeply troubled by an immoral war, the expanding, yawning gulf between the rich and the poor, and by the multitude of professed Christians who espouse war rather than peace? Amos, filled with the conviction and burden of God's word, did not hesitate to cry out against immorality and injustice. He sees no security in military might, in wealth, and in piety that is just for show. Amos's voice is as true today as it was in the eighth century before Christ. May we have ears to hear.

FOR REFLECTION

- Do people today believe in a God who is involved in contemporary history? What is the evidence of this?

- How do you think we understand the prophets today, as twenty-first-century Westerners? In avoiding "fire and brimstone" from the pulpit are we somehow ignoring the prophets and their warnings?

- Is there a responsibility for priests and pastors to speak against war and to draw judgments between the two extremes of wealth and poverty in a capitalistic society? Why do you think we hear so little commentary on this in church?

JOHN THE BAPTIZER:
ANOTHER VOICE CRYING IN THE WILDERNESS

Eight centuries separate the prophet Amos from the last of the great prophets of repentance; John the Baptizer appears after a long silence and prolonged darkness for the people of God. His message is as powerful as that of Amos. Amos, the truth-teller, was ignored by the comfortable and the powerful and had to return to his home knowing that he had done what God had commanded him but also sure that the people had not listened.

John calls for repentance, offers the gift of baptism, and is ready to relinquish his ministry to another whom he sees as the fulfillment of God's promise to God's people.

John the baptizer appeared in the wilderness, proclaiming a baptism of repentances for the forgiveness of sins.

(Mark 1:4)

What happened yesterday confirmed for me all of God's promises. And here I am now, taking a few moments to myself, trudging upstream alone, trying to calm the wild beating of my heart.

He came, he is real, I was not mistaken.

I had been waiting for him since my naming. That is my earliest memory: my father intoning the words of the prophets over my infant body. He said them so frequently as I was growing up that I was sure I had heard them in infancy; by the time I was weaned I could recite them as well as he.

And you, child, will be called the
prophet of the Most High;
for you will go before the Lord
to prepare his ways,
to give knowledge of salvation to
his people
for the forgiveness of their sins.

I was so sure of these words and these promises that I spent all my waking hours in preparation for the day when the Anointed of God would arrive. When my faithful, pious father died, I left the hill country to live in the wilderness, close to the water, close to the animals, sharing their food, dressing in their skins. I would tolerate nothing to be wasted in God's creation. I liked being alone, thinking, and saying aloud the words of the prophets that my good father taught me with diligence while I was living under his roof. And I found that when a man devotes himself to serving God and proclaiming God's truth, others follow. I didn't set out to find disciples; they found me.

We spend our days talking about the words of the prophets, reciting God's promises and God's admonitions, longing for the promised deliverance. They bring me news of the city, of the Roman soldiers, the corruption of Herod's palace, the complicity of the high priests. They remind me of what I have seen for myself—the poverty, the misery of the people of the villages, their hard lives. And I cry out to the Lord for the words to say to all of them.

The poor come to me for forgiveness, and I baptize them in the waters of the Jordan. "We are sorry for the wrongs we do to others," they say humbly, and I pronounce on them the forgiveness of the Lord who is always pleased with a heart that repents. The well-to-do come to me asking what they can do to find favor in God's eyes, and I tell them to share what they have with those who have nothing. When they clothe those who come in rags and give food to those who come to me hungry, I am glad to pronounce on them the Lord's forgiveness also, for God is pleased with a generous heart. Many of them decide to stay with me. They are hungry for God's words. They ask me, with longing, if I am the Anointed One, and always, always, I tell them the truth. "I came to prepare the way for the One who will baptize you with the Spirit of God," I tell them again and again. Together we have waited for the day of the Lord, for God's time.

But when the Pharisees and those who have some knowledge and some power come to see me, all they want of me is this: *We need to know who you are*, not because they are in favor of what I am doing but because they want to challenge me. "Are you Elijah?" they ask. "Are you Messiah, the prophet of God? If you are not—who gives you the authority to say what you are saying? Who gives you the authority to baptize?" Anger fills me at their hypocrisy. "You brood of vipers," I call them.

They have not dared do me any harm, because hundreds of followers surround me.

"We have the right to ask," they say, "because we are the descendants of Abraham." As if the rest of us are not! I see them as trees ready to be cut down, as chaff to be thrown in the fire. I cry out for them to repent of their sin and their pride.

The same occurred yesterday, but with a new intensity. The crowd grew restless and loud. Most sided with me, but others, afraid of the wrath of those who held the government in their hands, started having doubts. My disciples came closer to me; I sensed something strong in the air and like my friends, the animals, I shivered at what was coming; was it an earthquake? The noise stopped suddenly as a young man pushed through the crowd and said in a strong voice that had in it nothing of fear, a sure voice that revealed clearly to me that I was in the presence of authority. "John, my cousin, I want to be baptized by you."

"My cousin?" I whispered. I saw James-bar-Joseph with him and remembered that he had been my disciple for a short while; then memories of my childhood rushed at me. My mother telling me of her cousin Mary of Nazareth, of days of miracles and joy. I looked at the man in front of me and I knew him. I was in the presence of the one who was to come. *He is here, with me* I thought and I started trembling. "No, I told him, I am not worthy to baptize you. You should baptize *me*." But he looked at me as if to pass his great peace into my own body and he said, "John, I came to be baptized by you," and he entered the water. I turned to the crowd and cried out.

"Here he is! This is the one of whom I said, *Someone is coming after me whose sandals I am not worthy to untie.*"

A strong current seemed to fly over the water, and as I lifted Jesus up out of the river, and his head rose as high as mine, I heard strange sounds that made me tremble anew. I looked at the crowds, but they were oblivious. I stared at Jesus and his attention told me that he was listening. A dove perched on his head and the voice now was clear. "You are my Son, the Beloved; with you I am well pleased."

I started weeping but Jesus laid his hand on mine and smiled. "It is well," the smile said. "Rejoice, for you were chosen to hear these words also."

I begged him to stay with me the rest of the day, and he did. Early this morning he moved on to the wilderness to be by himself, and here I am trying to take it all in. How can I convey to the world that this is the One we have been waiting for?

Thinking about John

John the Baptizer stands in my mind as the ultimate in humbly accepting his God-given role. His advent was miraculous; his parents were filled with assurances from above; the Angel Gabriel visited his father as he visited the parents of Jesus. These stories must have been told to him since infancy.

He chooses the role of a *prodromos*—the one who goes before to open the way. He lives an ascetic, lean life. He is assiduous in the proclamation of repentance because he knows who he is and what is expected of him. Unlike most human beings who become famous and attract followers, he is not seduced by the crowds. He remains pure in his conviction, his humility, and his solitariness.

When Jesus approaches, John is at the height of his own power. Yet he immediately recognizes who Jesus is and points him out to his own disciples. In effect he is telling them, Jesus is the one you should follow. John diminishes as Jesus increases and he does so knowingly and willingly.

FOR REFLECTION

- Can you think of any famous person who reminds you of John? In what ways are they similar? How are they different?

- Can you think of anyone who gave up power and fame for the sake of another?

- What does John teach us about humility and self-negation in an age where we see how totally power corrupts?

❄ Words of Fulfillment

SECOND ISAIAH: A VOICE OF CONSOLATION

Do not remember the former
things,
or consider the things of old.
I am about to do a new thing;
now it springs forth, do you not
perceive it?

(Isaiah 43:18–19)

In the alien city of Babylon, everything I write sounds mournful to my ears, tinged by the unending sorrow of exile. Yet my people are accustomed to Babylon: they stroll its wide streets, they frequent the shops, they sit by running waters and hanging gardens pretending to belong. They are accustomed to exile—comfortable, content now to remain here. For me, residence in this alien land retains its bitterness, for I long for Zion; I always long for Zion.

The Babylonians revere me as poet, though I hide my work from them. Those few of my people who know me call me a prophet; others abuse me. Almost no one believes me. I know that I follow in the tradition of Isaiah, but after my years of proclamation I now hide in my study, see my visions, and write. The public forum is not for me. The quiet life of the spirit is what I have chosen as my lot, for the Lord has filled my ears with songs and my soul is overflowing with words that arrive accompanied by visions.

Cyrus the king sent an emissary who arrived in the dark. "We have been sent to bring you news of Cyrus's victories; he will destroy Babylon and you will be set free," he announces, but there is a price to be paid. I am to write in praise of Cyrus. I said to him, "I write only the words the Lord gives me. If the Lord speaks well of Cyrus, I will not hide it."

The time is coming when the people will be set free to return to Zion. I see the road opening before them and the vision is one of blessing and joy.

Every valley shall be exalted
and every mountain and hill made low.

They will return
in peace for
the grass withers, the flower
fades;
but the word of our God will
stand forever.

There was a traveler from Greece who came to Babylon for a time. He shared with me the poems of his people. "Athena stands by the Greeks," he told me, "and fights next to them, dressed in full battle array." I laughed at the image of the idol, for though my God "comes with might and his arm rules for him," there is another image that fills me and obliterates all others: "He shall feed his flock like a Shepherd; he will gather the lambs in his arms, and carry them in his bosom, and gently lead the mother sheep." Yahweh is a tender God; Yahweh is the Holy One. I hear his voice: "I am the Lord, and there is no other. I form light and create darkness, I make weal and create woe; I the Lord do all these things."

The words now come pouring forth. I cannot contain them. The visions are so painfully etched that I cry out to the Lord to keep me from the pain so that I have strength to write them down. I have read Isaiah again and again and marvel at his understanding—the recollection of God's past actions, the strong arm of the Lord upon the present—but it is the future that I see before me, for none of this has yet to pass. I ask the Lord to reveal to me who it is that I see, but I am before the Holy of Holies and I tremble. No clear answer arrives and none that I can reveal to those who read my words.

I see the Servant of Yahweh. I hear the words of the Servant and I see the one who lives and suffers as the Servant, but I can do nothing but repeat the words of this man of sorrows. "Despised and rejected of men," he is indeed. Whips and lashes have opened wounds on his back, and his face has been torn like that of a hunted animal.

The Lord God has opened my ear,
and I was not rebellious
I did not turn backward.
I gave my back to those who
struck me
and my cheeks to those who
pulled out the beard;
I did not hide my face
from insult and spitting. . . .

The people turn their faces from him, and yet he opens
not his mouth. He is bent over by the weight of the crowd's
sin, and I know that he does so willingly.

Surely he has borne our griefs
and carried our sorrows
yet we accounted him stricken,
struck down by God, and
afflicted.
But he was wounded for our
transgressions,
crushed for our iniquities;
upon him was the punishment that
made us whole;
and by his bruises we are
healed.

Who will choose this role for himself? I urgently ask of the
Lord. And all I receive in response is the unfathomable sorrow of a father. I tremble.

He was oppressed, and he was
afflicted,
yet he did not open his mouth;
like a lamb that is led to the slaughter,
and like a sheep that before its
shearers is silent,
so he did not open his mouth. . . .
he was cut off from the land
of the living,
stricken for the transgression of
my people.

I cannot endure any more of such suffering, for I recognize
it in myself. I too made myself a mediator between my people
and Yahweh, but my anguish has been as nothing before that
of the Lord's Servant. *Is it Moses?* I ask, as I am remember-
ing the promise of a new Moses. I persevere. I do not emerge
from my room for days. Silence offers some relief. Then I hear
again the voice I recognize, now a voice of assurance:

The Lord called me before I
was born,
while I was in my mother's
womb he named me.
He made my mouth like a sharp
sword,
in the shadow of his hand he
hid me;
he made me a polished arrow
in his quiver he hid me away. . . .

I will give you as a light to the nations,
that my salvation may reach to
the end of the earth.

I am beginning to hope that all is not lost for God's Servant. He gives himself willingly to untold pain, confident, despite all, that God is with him. This prophet I see in my vision is a prophet sent for the whole world, all nations. It is only Yahweh's word that can bring this to pass: *that one can suffer in the place of many.* Yahweh is pleased with his Servant:

See my servant shall prosper;
he shall be exalted and lifted up
and shall be very high. . . .

I see him clearly: a man, a prophet, a Servant. He is the One who shall come to save not only Israel but the whole world. When, O Lord, when? There is no answer set in a time that I foresee for myself. Yet, I know that he shall come. At the fullness of time, he shall come. He, indeed, is the fulfillment of Yahweh's promise.

Thinking about Second Isaiah

[T]he claim of Jesus as messiah was made and was found by many to be compelling. The linkage, however, is all necessarily made on the *fulfillment end* of the bridge of promise and fulfillment . . . it is *Christian* interpretive work to claim the promise for Jesus.[20]

For the field within which all these texts are inter-
preted extends from the time when the events they
contain were first recorded to their final interpretation
in the light of the saving event of Christ's coming. The
theological term "prediction" is, after all, simply the
discovery that the message of the ancient words holds
good right down to the time of Christ and, indeed,
that their true message only, becomes apparent when
they are applied to him.[21]

The Spirit of the Lord is upon
me,
because he has anointed me
to bring good news to the
poor.
He has sent me to
proclaim release
to the captives
and recovery of sight to the
blind,
to let the oppressed go free,
to proclaim the year of the Lord's
favor.

(Luke 4:18–19)

Who is this remarkable poet/prophet? Unlike Isaiah
of Jerusalem who gives us some autobiographical clues, we
know nothing about the prophet that scholars call Deutero-
Isaiah (from the Greek *deuteros,* second), for we have no
other name for him.

The first thirty-nine chapters of Isaiah were written by a distinct hand (and voice) in the eighth century BCE, before the Babylonian exile. The rest of the book, especially chapters 40–55, carry the imprint of this unknown master of metaphors, of exultation, and visions. On chapters 56–66 there is not much agreement concerning authorship. Portions of these chapters, especially 60–62, sound very much like Deutero-Isaiah. Several chapters seem to know the historical events around 400 BCE, so they may have been written by disciples, much later. I am more concerned with Second Isaiah and the Servant Songs, for I am convinced that Jesus made them his own, in his life and suffering. We cannot possibly know whom the prophet had in mind when he wrote these songs. "This transcendence of all familiar human categories is characteristic of discourse which foretells the future."[22] Gerhard von Rad is convinced that the Servant Songs are predictive and that they do not refer to a king but to a prophet: "The Servant's function is either that of a king or that of a prophet. On my judgment, only the second of these can be correct."[23]

As a confessing Christian, I see that what Second Isaiah foresaw about the return of the exiles and the flowering desert and easy highway of return did not come to pass. The segments that were fulfilled are those of the Servant Songs. But this is the Christian interpretation: we can't be sure of who and what the prophet was seeing when he wrote about the Suffering Servant. Brueggemann wrote, "Old Testament theology, it seems to me, may acknowledge the linkage made to Jesus but may at the same time wonder about the exclusiveness of the claim, since it is in the nature of the Old Testament witness to allow for other historically designated agents to do Yahweh's work of justice and righteousness in the earth,"[24] and

I have no difficulty with this. It seems to agree with von Rad's conclusion: "The tremendous new factor which he (Deutero-Isaiah) introduced—and it goes far beyond all previous prophecy—was the universal sweep of this prediction."[25]

For me it is all glorious and logical. It makes great sense. I have approached Deutero-Isaiah with fear and trembling but also with faith. I do not assume that prophecy, by its nature, predicts the future; but in this case, it is evident that the Suffering Servant is not a person of the past, and it is difficult to see who would be the subject of Deutero-Isaiah's contemporary world. It has to be someone *who is to come*. I do not think that the prophet saw Jesus of Nazareth in his visions, but someone who resembled Jesus in the life he led and the sacrifice he was willing to offer of himself. For this I am eternally grateful.

FOR REFLECTION

Read the Servant Songs and chapters 40–56 for their poetry and their conviction that God is savior and protector.

- What images of the Servant do you see embodied in Jesus of Nazareth?

- Do you think it was inevitable for the early church to see the connection between the Old Testament and the New?

MARY THE MOTHER: A VOICE OF JUSTICE

I dwell in the high and holy place,
and also with those who are
contrite and humble in
spirit,
to revive the spirit of the humble,
and to revive the heart of the contrite.

(Isaiah 57:15b)

When I was still a child, my father told me that the God of Israel is a God of justice. The God of Israel is holy and righteous, he added. I did not understand the words but I felt them.

Our hilly Nazareth was very poor. We managed to survive— that is all.

We saw few Romans passing through. They much preferred large Sepphoris and Tiberias, the rich cities. What little we saw of Romans, we did not like. They were frightening in their armor, their short tunics, their arrogant faces; even their horses seemed superior to us. Horses and soldiers, both, looked down on us poor, occupied Jews. But we had more urgent needs to worry us. Our neighbors said that they felt forgotten by God.

My father, like the other men of the village, worked on the hard soil that produced just enough for us to eat; he also looked after a couple of sheep and lambs, reserved for special occasions and for times of drought and famine. My mother worked in and around the house from sunup to sundown, and I learned early on to help her so that she would not be exhausted at night and grow old before her time.

Nazareth was also beautiful. I often stood on our rocky yard, looking across the low dip of the land in the middle to the circle of hills that surrounded it, all the while thinking of the words of psalms. I waited for the light to reveal the distant horizon with a pink hue that pleased my soul. Then in the evening I followed the sun's path to the west, marveling at the deep red of the light, the spreading color so vivid that it has remained in my memory forever. I was both dreamy and practical, Mother said, and I agreed. I spent my quiet hours alone in the yard, or in the field when I helped Father, thinking about all I heard and saw, praying to God, the Holy One, and listening for a voice that I had recognized every now and then as being outside the human realm of our village. I loved the sound of that voice and the secrets it revealed to me.

When Gabriel, the blessed, appeared to me I knew that I had heard his voice before, for I recognized it. The nine months I carried my child in my womb, I became familiar with the voice that revealed and commanded. Later, it stopped visiting me. I thought for a while that Jesus had supplanted that voice, and I know now that this was true, but I wasn't sure at that time.

I was absolutely certain that it visited me most fully when I met Elizabeth for the first time.

Before I started showing that I was with child, I left Nazareth for the hills of Judea, in the south. Our village was small, and since I was not yet married, the gossip would upset my parents. With their urging, I agreed to travel to my cousin's home. My father found a caravan going south; he entrusted me to an old friend, and I traveled with them to a land I did not know. The hills were rolling and more gentle than ours and the vegetation in some places was lush. We bypassed Jerusalem and I left the caravan to follow the climbing path to Elizabeth's home.

I was young and strong and eager to meet the priest Zechariah and his wife.

I approached their house, coming uphill, seeing the flat roof first and then the open door and Elizabeth framed against the light, a woman like my mother, but showing that she too was with child. She turned and looked full at me, and then she sped toward me. I dropped my bundle to embrace her and saw that she was deeply moved. Her voice rose and surprised me both with the words and their strength.

"Blessed are you among women and blessed is the fruit of your womb," she cried. And then she called me the mother of her Lord, which really stunned me. "Feel," she said, and placed my hand on her belly. "The child is dancing in my womb at your approach." Elizabeth looked into my eyes. "Ah, Mary, you believed in the Lord's promise; you are blessed."

And then the voice spoke through me. I was no longer surprised. I threw my arms above my head and cried to the heavens,

> My soul magnifies the Lord,
> and my spirit rejoices in God
> my Savior,
> for he has looked with favor on
> the lowliness of his servant.
> Surely from now on all
> generations will call
> me blessed;

for the Mighty One has done
great things for me,
and holy is his name.

Elizabeth was weeping and smiling and nodding. She agreed. Here we were, two women dressed in the simplest clothes—homespun, rough weave—she in house slippers, I in worn-out sandals, agreeing that we were blessed, that we would be blessed unto eternity, convinced that God had looked at us with favor. We were not forgotten by God. The promised "great things" of God were here. And they were not reserved for the powerful and the wise but for us, poor village women waiting for our babes to arrive. The voice again filled me.

His mercy is for those who fear him
from generation to generation.

I knew this kind of fear; I felt it at Gabriel's appearance, at the promise of a child to me when I knew no man. A fear like tremendous love mixed with awe and wonder, with the Holy. God's mercy was not reserved for the world's leaders or for those who knew how to read and speak in the synagogue; it was for all of us who felt the presence of God. And I knew at that moment what a great truth I had discovered. This woman before me and her quiet husband standing near us now and watching us in silence—these people were more important in God's eyes than the proud Romans and the high priests, all of them demanding taxes from us, the poor.

He has shown strength with
 his arm;
he has scattered the proud in the
thoughts of their hearts.
He has brought down the
powerful from their
thrones,
and lifted up the lowly.

And I knew that it was God who was revealing all this to
me. I saw human pride for what it was and human glory with
all its passing futility. Hunger was a constant accompaniment
to the lives of the poor, and I longed for the next words:

He has filled the hungry with
good things,
and sent the rich away empty.

I knew that this was more than food for the body, but
how important it is to have enough to eat! I would go back to
Nazareth to tell them that God has not forgotten us; I would
teach all this to my son; I would see that children were fed. I
remembered the God of promises to us since time immemo-
rial, the God of justice:

He has helped his servant Israel,
in remembrance of his mercy,
according to the promise he made
to our ancestors,
to Abraham and to his
descendants forever.

I stopped and looked at Elizabeth and Zechariah. He picked up my bundle and she put her arm around me to lead me under their roof.

"The hour has come," Elizabeth said. "Now that you are here, we know that God's time of fulfillment has arrived."

We spent three good months together. I learned much from Elizabeth as we walked and worked together. She was a woman of experience and deep faith and she taught me what she knew of the Scriptures and of God. Her deep humility touched me to the core of my being—her conviction that her son would lead the way for mine. I was the younger but she bent and kissed my hand. I have never forgotten those hours with the good woman who became John's mother.

I have never forgotten the voice that revealed to me what my father had told me as a child: the God of promises is a God of justice. The Son I was carrying would reveal to us a God of love.

FOR REFLECTION

Let's look carefully at the Magnificat, Mary's magnificent hymn, and the ways it relates to issues of justice that concern us today.

- What contemporary injustices do you see mirrored in the Magnificat?

- In Mary's words, there is a "preferential order" for the poor. Discuss what this means to you individually. What do you think it means to us in our communities? In our nations? In the larger world?

The Logos: an Epilogue

When I was a child I wrote a novel centered on John, the beloved disciple. My interest in him dates from that early time. Later, among my husband's books, I discovered Archbishop William Temple's superb *Readings in St. John's Gospel*, and my love increased and was confirmed.

Years later, on a sad day when I traveled with a friend to Black Mountain in North Carolina to visit her dying father, who was a minister in the Disciples Church, I was asked by him to read the prologue to John's Gospel aloud in Greek. It remains one of my sacred memories in its connection to my friend, her dying father, and John. I wrote in John's voice only once before in *Walking the Way of Sorrows: Stations of the Cross*.[26] I want the following monologue to serve as the epilogue to this volume.

THE LOGOS

I had known him so well as my friend and teacher, the human Jesus of laughter and energy, the devoted friend who tolerated no pretensions or arrogance. He saw through us. We could hide nothing from him. James and I had been such close friends, more than brothers, and had prided ourselves in hiding our thoughts from others. But we could hide nothing from our beloved Jesus. He loved us, but he also called us *Boanerges*, "sons of thunder," for our ambition and our arguments with the rest of the disciples. Those happy years spent with him were the years of unqualified joy for us. His death shattered us, came close to destroying us, but for the hope that life like his could not be extinguished. Not if there was a God, and he had assured us that there was a God who loved us. He had never lied to us, so I lived in hope, though I wept at his loss for every hour of those last three days.

When Mary the Magdalene came to us that first day of the week to tell us that the body of our beloved Master had disappeared from the tomb, the beginning of everything new saw its dawn for me and for the others. I knew I would see him again, and when he appeared to us in that new resurrected reality of his, though I missed his former presence, I was convinced that my life would be spent for him from that moment on.

How many moments have passed into eternity since then. I am so old now, I can hardly see my own hand, much less the quill with which to write. So thank you, my young friend, for your strong eyes and your facile hand. We will write the story together: I will speak and you will put it down for all to read.

His reality came to me not in a flash but in a steady, increasing light of awareness and belief. I knew him as my friend and teacher, and now I know him as my Lord, the Bread of life, the Living Water, the Light of the world, the Door through whom we enter to the Father, the Good Shepherd, the Logos of God. When did I know that he was one with the Father? When did I know that he came from God but was God himself, that he was with God at the creation? I cannot pinpoint the time, but I can testify to my belief in all these qualities of the glorified Christ.

They are all gone now. My dear brother was the first of us to be killed for the sake of the Lord. How I have missed him. Then years later word reached me of the death of Peter, my fearless friend who was not fearless at the beginning but became the Rock as the Lord had promised. And so many others I have loved and lost. I have outlived them all, even that latecomer to us, the brilliant Paul who wrote the letters that endure. All of them have gone to the bosom of the Father, and I am ready to follow. I have been ready for a long time, but the word of God came to me that all this must be taken down, written, and saved before I can join them. So, listen carefully, my friend, and write down what I dictate. I praise the name of him who claimed me for his own. Now write:

In the beginning was the Logos, and the Logos was next to God, and God was Logos. It was he who was in the beginning with God. All things through him were created, and without him not one thing was created. In him was life, and life was the light of human beings. And the light shines in the darkness and the darkness did not extinguish it. . . .

Amen.

Notes

1. *The Man Born to Be King: A Play Cycle on the Life of Our Lord and Saviour Jesus Christ* (1943; repr., Grand Rapids: Eerdmans, 1974), 1.

2. Ibid., 3.

3. Ibid.

4. Gerhard von Rad, *Genesis: A Commentary* (Philadelphia: Westminster Press, 1972), 96.

5. Ibid., 47.

6. Author's translation directly from the Septuagint (Gen 1:26–27).

7. Carol Meyers, ed., *Women in Scripture* (Boston: Houghton Mifflin, 2000), 82.

8. von Rad, *Genesis*, 160.

9. Phyllis Trible, "Miriam 1," in *Women in Scripture*, 127–28.

10. See the chapter entitled "Jealous of God's Favor," 71–77.

11. Walter Brueggemann, *Theology of the Old Testament: Testimony, Dispute, Advocacy* (Minneapolis: Fortress, 1997), 325–26.

12. Katerina Katsarka Whitley, *Speaking for Ourselves: Voices of Biblical Women* (Harrisburg, PA: Morehouse Publishing, 1998).

13. Brueggemann, *Theology of the Old Testament*, 367.

14. Ibid., 370.

15. See "Is He Only a God of War?" in *Speaking for Ourselves*, 97–106.

16. von Rad, *Old Testament Theology*, vol. 2, *The Theology of Israel's Prophetic Traditions*, 145.

17. For a fuller interpretation, please see Elizabeth's monologue, "The dance in the womb" in Whitley, *Speaking for Ourselves*, 35–41, and Zechariah's "The Visitation" in Whitley, *Waiting for the Wonder*, 29–31.

18. Author's own verse.

19. Phyllis Trible, *Texts of Terror: Feminist Readings of Biblical Narratives* (Philadelphia: Fortress, 1984), 8.

20. Brueggemann, *Theology of the Old Testament,* 620; emphasis added.

21. von Rad, *Old Testament Theology,* vol. 2, *The Theology of Israel's Prophetic Traditions*, 384.

22. Ibid., 258.

23. Ibid., 259.

24. Brueggemann, *Theology of the Old Testament,* 620.

25. von Rad, *Old Testament Theology,* vol. 2, *The Theology of Israel's Prophetic Traditions*, 262.

26. Whitley, *Walking the Way of Sorrows: Stations of the Cross* (Harrisburg, PA: Morehouse Publishing, 2004), 15–17.

Bibliography

Brueggemann, Walter. *Theology of the Old Testament: Testimony, Dispute, Advocacy.* Minneapolis: Fortress, 1997.

Buttrick, George Arthur, ed. *The Interpreter's Dictionary of the Bible.* Vols. 1–4. Nashville: Abingdon, 1962.

Meyers, Carol, ed. *Women in Scripture.* Boston: Houghton Mifflin, 2000.

The New Oxford Annotated Bible with the Apocrypha: New Revised Standard Version. New York: Oxford University Press, 1991.

Rahlfs, Alfred, ed. *Septuaginta. Septuagint: The Old Testament in Greek.* Stuttgart, Germany: Deutsche Biblegesellschaft, 2006.

Sayers, Dorothy L. *The Man Born to Be King: A Play Cycle on the Life of our Lord and Saviour Jesus Christ.* 1943; repr., Grand Rapids: Eerdmans, 1974.

Trible, Phyllis. *Texts of Terror: Feminist Readings of Biblical Narratives.* Philadelphia: Fortress, 1984.

Von Rad, Gerhard. *Genesis: A Commentary.* Philadelphia: Westminster Press, 1972.

———. *Old Testament Theology.* Vol. 1, *The Theology of Israel's Historical Traditions.* New York: Harper & Row, 1962.

———. *Old Testament Theology.* Vol. 2, *The Theology of Israel's Prophetic Traditions.* New York: Harper & Row, 1965.

Whitley, Katerina Katsarka. *Speaking for Ourselves: Voices of Biblical Women.* Harrisburg, PA: Morehouse Publishing, 1998.

———. *Waiting for the Wonder: Voices of Advent.* Harrisburg, PA: Morehouse Publishing, 2005.

———. *Walking the Way of Sorrows: Stations of the Cross.* Harrisburg, PA: Morehouse Publishing, 2004.